SINATRA

SINATRA

A Life in Music

LEW IRWIN

Friedman Group

A FRIEDMAN GROUP BOOK

© 1995 by Michael Friedman Publishing Group, Inc.

ISBN 1-56799-221-8

SINATRA
A Life in Music
was prepared and produced by
Michael Friedman Publishing Group, Inc.
15 West 26th Street
New York, New York 10010

Editor: Benjamin Boyington
Art Director: Jeff Batzli
Designer: Lynne Yeamans
Photography Editor: Colleen A. Branigan

Color separations by Bright Arts (Singapore) Pte Ltd.
Printed in China by Leefung-Asco Printers Ltd.

Photography Credits

AP/Wide World Photo: 41, 42, 52, 75, 97, 101, 106; © Ron Frehm/AP: 111
Archive Photos: 9, 10, 12 (bottom), 18, 26 (left), 32, 34, 35, 47 (both), 49 (left), 51, 53, 54, 55, 56, 57, 58, 69, 70, 74, 76, 77, 78 (right), 82, 83, 84
The Bettmann Archive: 29, 30 (left)
Frank Driggs Collection: 11, 22 (both), 30 (right), 37
The Everett Collection: 13, 15, 20, 24, 33, 36, 38, 40, 45 (left), 50, 61 (left), 64, 66, 71, 80, 88, 91, 92
FPG: 28 (right), 72, 109
Globe Photos: 26 (right), 39, 94, 104; © Ray Johnson/Camera Press/Globe: 107; SMP/Globe: 90, 105
Lester Glassner Collection: 6, 12 (top), 17, 25, 44, 49 (right), 62
Neal Peters: 2, 7, 8, 21, 63, 93, 96;
    © Frank Teti/Neal Peters Collection: 108, 112
Photofest: 27, 28 (left), 45 (right), 46, 48, 59, 65, 67, 68, 78 (left), 79, 81, 100, 102, 103
Retna: ©Bob Willoughby/Redferns/Retna: 86, 87, 99
Star File Photos: 16
UPI/Bettmann: 14, 19, 23, 31, 43, 60, 61 (right)

Dedication

To my daughter, Sara.
You gotta have high hopes!

Acknowledgments

The author gratefully acknowledges the staff of the Margaret Herrick Library of the Academy of Motion Picture Arts and Sciences Center for Motion Picture Study, Beverly Hills, California, for their assistance and contributions in the preparation of this book.

Much of the text material, some of which is published here for the first time, is derived from papers and notes archived in the academy library. These include the personal papers and files of columnists Hedda Hopper and Sidney Skolsky and director Fred Zinneman; the files of the Production Code Administration; the annual reports of the California Senate Special Committee on Un-American Activities from the years 1947 to 1950; and original manuscripts, some unpublished, submitted by writers to *Photoplay* and other fan magazines in the 1940s and 1950s.

This book deals primarily with Frank Sinatra's unparalleled contributions to American popular culture. His public life was of course affected by his personal life, and because of that fact, there are numerous references to intimate matters that most individuals would choose to keep private. These references are not intended to subject Mr. Sinatra to further embarrassment, but rather to shed some light on the driving mechanism behind his compelling talent.

Some of this book is based on an extensive interview with Frank Sinatra recorded by the author in November 1981 for the nationally syndicated radio program *Earth News Radio*. Mr. Sinatra, through his publicist, rejected a request by the author for a further interview in connection with this book. "When Mr. Sinatra wants the story of his life to be published," she said, "he will tell it himself." Such a book will be eagerly awaited by Mr. Sinatra's legions of fans, but it is my opinion that he himself may be surprised by some of the information assembled here about the influence of others upon his career.

This book does not profess to be a definitive biography. It is my hope, however, that it will serve to help illuminate the personality and accomplishments of a remarkable individual, and that it may inspire others to emulate his example: to strive—fight, even—for excellence, despite the foibles that bedevil us all.

CONTENTS

The Early Years

*O**pposite:** The young Sinatra was famous for his disarming smile and charming bluntness. **Left:** A family photo of the teenage Frank ☆*

Hoboken

Hoboken, New Jersey, which lies in the shadow of New York City on the western banks of the Hudson River, has always been a tough, gritty port town. Kids growing up there either resign themselves to its dreariness or dream of escaping it. The son of Anthony Martin Sinatra, the proprietor of a tavern, and Natalie "Dolly" Sinatra, a

Democratic Party district leader, Frank Sinatra lived the first third of his life in Hoboken.

He was a scrapper from birth, so large—twelve and three-quarter pounds—that he had to be pulled out of his ninety-pound mother with medical forceps that scarred his face, one ear, and his neck (Sinatra had these scars removed when he was in his sixties). Delivered in the bedroom of the Sinatra apartment, the baby was at first pronounced stillborn and set aside by the doctor while he worked to save the life of the mother. But, as neighborhood women who had gathered around shrieked and wept, Dolly's mother plucked up the baby, carried him into the bathroom, and held him under the cold-water faucet. A moment later, Francis Albert Sinatra wailed for the first time. It was December 12, 1915.

Sinatra grew up in a middle-class neighborhood bordering an area of grimy tenements and factories. His parents and relatives doted on him, spoiled him. His teachers would recall later that he was always a show-off, and often disruptive in class. His father, a bantamweight who boxed professionally for a time under the name Marty O'Brien, taught young Frankie at an early age how to use his fists.

"In my particular neighborhood of New Jersey when I was a kid," Sinatra once said, "boys became boxers or they worked in factories, and then the remaining group that I went around with were smitten by singing. I mean, we had a ukulele player, and we'd stand on the corner and sing songs."

Others were standing on corners selling apples in those days. Sinatra was thirteen years old when the market crashed in 1929. Poverty was the national condition. But you wouldn't know it from the popular music of the times, which was generally upbeat both musically and lyrically—probably at no other time was the word "smile" used so often in song.

Frank's mother used her Democratic Party connections to good advantage. By Hoboken standards, the Sinatra family appeared downright prosperous. In 1931 they were even able to move into a new home that sported a central heating system. In his room Frank collected and displayed pictures of singers and movie stars—Al Jolson, Rudy Vallee, Bing Crosby—and he began trying to affect their look and style, earning a reputation among his school chums as a snappy dresser.

At Demarest High School, Sinatra helped form a glee club and played in the school band. After school, he boxed at the Park Athletic Club and joined the Tommy Carey Association, an athletic organization named after a St. Louis Browns shortstop from

Opposite: Martin Anthony Sinatra and Natalie "Dolly" (née Garavanti) on their wedding day, February 14, 1914. **Left:** *Even at the age of three, Frank was a dashing young rake.*

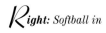

Right: Softball in hand, adolescent Frankie pauses from play to pose for the camera. Even at this age, he was already a natural charmer.

Below: *A very young Frank Sinatra (front row, far right) with family and friends in the Catskills in June 1923.*

Hoboken. Frank somehow got the idea that athletics would strengthen his voice. He spent hours swimming and timing himself underwater, believing that the training was great conditioning for sustaining notes.

By the time he was fifteen he was telling everyone he knew that he had decided to become a singer. This ambition horrified his parents, even though the one "rich and famous" relative in the family was a cousin, Ray Sinatra, who conducted a band at some of Broadway's most celebrated venues. Marty Sinatra figured his son had boxing talent, and Dolly wanted him to become a businessman. Frank quit Demarest in his sophomore year and entered Drake Institute, a local business school, where he stayed only a few months—until he was sixteen, the legal age for dropping out of school in New Jersey.

In the summer of 1932 he accompanied his parents to their summer place in Long Branch, New Jersey. There he met fifteen-year-old Nancy Barbato, who came from Jersey City and lived across the street with her family. The two teenagers fell in love. In a March 1943 article for a magazine with the sentimental and redundant title of *Love Romances*, Nancy, in an as-told-to article with Gladys Hall, recalled, "Our crowd laughed at us for being so immediately and entirely absorbed one with the other. They said, 'Summer

romances never last.' It never mattered to us what people said. Our hearts did the only talking to which we listened." They continued dating after the summer was over.

According to Nancy, "Frank didn't sing much then.... Now and then when we went to a dance he'd sing for the girls and boys, but just very casually. I think 'Learn to Croon' was the first song I ever heard him sing. We spent most of our dates...listening to [Bing Crosby's] songs. We admired him very much...and we always knew the lyrics to every song."

One day in 1933, the seventeen-year-old Frank took Nancy to a local vaudeville theater to see Crosby perform. What made the show particularly memorable for him was that, as Sinatra recalls, it was Crosby's last vaudeville appearance. "He never appeared in person after that anymore—on anybody's stage. And I was dating Nancy at the time, and we went to see him, and I thought, 'Well, it seems so easy.' He was working with a guitarist, just a guitarist, no orchestra. And I thought to myself, 'If he can do that, why can't I do that?'"

Nancy recalled in her article in *Love Romances*: "I never felt anyone sit so still as Frank did that evening. When we came out of the theater, he said, 'That is what I want to do.'"

Meanwhile, Sinatra got an eleven-dollar-a-week job working on the news truck of the *Jersey Observer*, saving some of the money to buy a car and spending the rest on clothes. Years later he would tell interviewers that he also hung out with aspiring toughs who were working themselves up from stealing candy to stealing bicycles. One of them would become the notorious capo Willie Moretti. Inevitably, he had his share of run-ins with police, sometimes arriving home bruised and bloodied from beatings at the local station house, where, he told his parents, police had interrogated him about how he had come by the money for his shiny car and sporty attire.

In 1934 he was hired as a copy boy for the *Observer*, shuffling papers in the sports department. A year later, he was covering college sports events. He might have wound up writing the news instead of starring in it had he not landed an appearance on *The Major Bowes Original Amateur Hour*, a national radio program, with a trio from Hoboken that included Jimmy Petrozelli ("Skelly"), Patty Principe ("Patty Prince"), and Fred Tamburro ("Tamby"). It was Bowes himself who teamed Sinatra with the street-corner singers from his neighborhood. They had auditioned separately for the show but, Sinatra later related, when the auditions were over Bowes summoned them together and remarked, "Why don't we put you on together, and we'll call [you] the Hoboken four?"

"Around and Around She Goes"

In 1934 *The Major Bowes Original Amateur Hour* was the most popular radio show in the United States. The careers of countless entertainers were launched on this program. "Around and around she goes and where she stops nobody knows," Major Edward Bowes would intone at the beginning of every program each week as audiences heard the sound of a spinning roulette wheel—"the wheel of fortune," Bowes called it.

At the time, Bowes was receiving ten thousand applications a week from would-be contestants—most of whom had been hit hard by the Depression—who hoped to win big at his "wheel."

Piano players, washboard players, spoon players, singers, comics, and tap dancers applied. Many didn't wait for replies. They streamed into New York by the trainload. In one week alone in 1935, *Newsweek* reported, fifteen hundred amateur performers applied for emergency food and shelter in New York City. Bowes, in an effort to avoid blame for increasing the burden on the city's already overburdened welfare system, announced that only applicants already residing in the New York area would be eligible to become contestants on his program. Luckily for the eager quartet, Hoboken was apparently just within this boundary.

A recording of the Hoboken Four's initial *Amateur Hour* appearance—they sang "Shine," accompanied by a ukulele—still

Major Edward Bowes, flanked by the Hoboken Four (Frankie is on the far right).

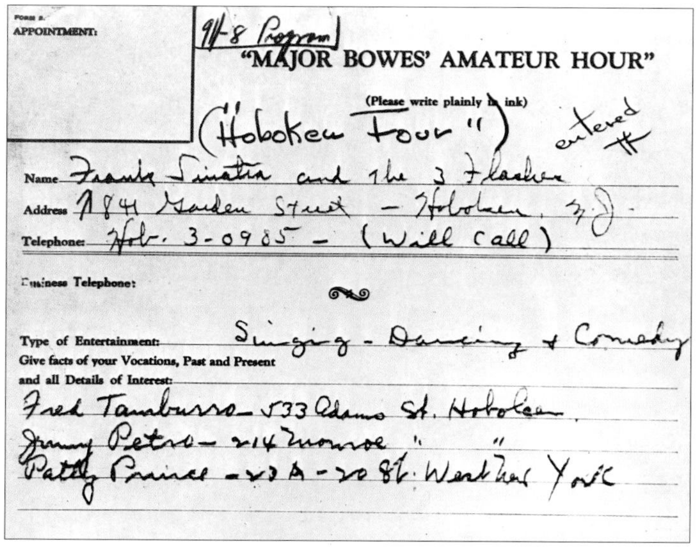

The handwritten form reads:

FORM A.
APPOINTMENT: "MAJOR BOWES' AMATEUR HOUR"

(Please write plainly in ink)

("Hoboken Four") entered #

Name Frank Sinatra and the 3 Flashes
Address 184 Garden Street – Hoboken, N.J.
Telephone: Hob. 3-0985 – (Will call)

Business Telephone:

Type of Entertainment: Singing – Dancing + Comedy
Give facts of your Vocations, Past and Present and all Details of Interest:
Fred Tamburro – 533 Adams St. Hoboken.
Jimmy Petro – 214 Monroe " "
Patty Prince – 23A – 20 St. West New York

exists. If one listens to this recording, it becomes clear that the group must have had something going for them other than musical talent because they sound so painfully amateur. What they did have in abundance was a youthful appeal that charmed the venerable Bowes.

"They seem so happy, I guess," Bowes remarked on the air after their performance, "and [they make] everybody else happy." Bowes then asked each of the members of the group what they did for a living, but was interrupted when one of them pointed at his skinny colleague and remarked, "And this fellow over here never works at all." Bowes chuckled.

"I'm Frank, Major," said Sinatra, neatly taking his cue. "We're looking for jobs. How about it? Everybody that's ever heard us likes us. We think we're pretty good."

In fact, they were pretty awful, despite the fifty dollars and the first prize they were awarded at the end of the show. But Bowes did have a job for them. He first signed them to a one-week engagement at the Roxy theater, then put them in an *Amateur Hour* touring company and sent them on the road for three months. Every night the Hoboken Four would perform in a different vaudeville house, doing their best to sound like the number one singer of the day, Bing Crosby. All except the skinny kid.

"I was the only one in my neighborhood, [the only one] of the young kids anywhere in my home town, who had aspirations to sound different," Sinatra says. "They were all copying what Bing was doing with his sound. And I didn't want to do that. I wanted something else. I didn't know what I wanted, but I didn't want to do that, just because everybody was going to be a Crosby."

Bing Crosby was, in fact, the very first major recording star, cutting his first solo record in 1927. To be sure, there had been fine performers before him who sang on records—Al Jolson, Rudy Vallee, and Eddie Cantor were some of the most popular—but Crosby was the first to sing primarily for people gathered around phonographs in their own homes. He was the first to make the relationship between the singer and his listeners an intimate one.

Crosby was doing it *all* back then, everything from jazz to Viennese waltzes, Beiderbecke to Friml. Jack Kapp, who had signed Crosby at Brunswick, produced his early records and made certain they delivered something to everybody. Sinatra's parents loved Crosby's records, and so did he.

"There weren't a lot of singers to listen to. I listened to Bing constantly. I had all of his records, and I was a big fan, really a gigantic fan, of his."

I N THE EARLY 1930s BING CROSBY HAD ONLY ONE RIVAL, A ONE-TIME OPERA SINGER NAMED RUSS COLUMBO. THE TWO WAGED WHAT WAS CALLED "THE BATTLE OF THE BARITONES" ON THE RADIO, CROSBY ON CBS, COLUMBO ON NBC. COLUMBO'S GREATEST ASSET, HOWEVER, MAY NOT HAVE BEEN HIS VOICE, BUT HIS LOOKS. CLASSICALLY HANDSOME, HE BORE A STRIKING RESEMBLANCE TO RUDOLPH VALENTINO. HE APPEARED IN TWO MOVIES AND STARRED IN A THIRD, *WAKE UP AND DREAM*, AND WOMEN WHO HEARD HIM ON RECORDS AND SAW HIM IN THE MOVIES POURED OUT THEIR LOVE FOR HIM IN THOUSANDS OF FAN LETTERS EVERY WEEK. BUT THE RIVALRY BETWEEN CROSBY AND COLUMBO ENDED IN 1934 WHEN COLUMBO WAS KILLED IN A FATAL GUN ACCIDENT.☆

"Back then there were only two singers, Bing and Russ Columbo," Sinatra once said, "and when Columbo was unfortunately killed in Hollywood, Bing was the only man around who was still recording."

Yet it really wasn't Crosby's vocal style that aroused Sinatra's ambitions to become a singer. It was his wealth. As Sinatra put it: "Crosby influenced me, I think, by his success. Because he was such an easy-going performer that when I first saw him on the stage that time, I thought to myself, 'That's not too tough to do.' [But] it took me twenty-five years to get to where he was at that point."

The program summary card for the Hoboken Four's entry on The Major Bowes Amateur Hour.☆

On The Air

On a night out

with his mom and dad.

The gleam of Marty's

buttons is matched

only by the shine of

Frank's pearly whites.

During his street-corner singing days, Sinatra had to croon into a small megaphone to project a voice that sounded about as thin and weak as he looked. Other performers knew how to amplify their voices naturally. Even Crosby could be heard distinctly at the back of an auditorium with a band playing behind him. Sinatra, however, couldn't project his voice—he would have made a lousy vaudevillian. But his *Amateur Hour* experience revealed to him the virtues of the microphone. He saw that with this device he could project his voice not only across a theater, but across the country (and even the world).

After his appearance on the *Amateur Hour*, Sinatra was easily able to land a few fifteen-dollar-a-week emcee and singing jobs in taverns and roadhouses around New York. Later on, there were suggestions that the owners of these places, many of them former Depression-era gangsters who had converted speakeasies into legitimate saloons, had taken a special liking to Sinatra. Willie Moretti, at the time a low-rung gangster, was particularly helpful in getting him work.

But what Sinatra was really looking for was a place that had a "wire," a link to a radio station. His mother, Dolly, found just the right place for him at a roadhouse in Englewood, New Jersey, in 1939. He sang vocals with Harry Arden's band, emceed the night's entertainment, and got paid twenty-five dollars a week. And he was on the air on WNEW New York every night.

"I was working with an orchestra at the Rustic Cabin, six nights a week, from seven-thirty in the evening until four in the morning," Sinatra recalls. For him, at age twenty-three, the work was exhilarating. "That was what I wanted to do. I wanted to get the actual, physical work done every night, so that I could experiment. I couldn't have paid for that experience."

It was while he was performing at the Rustic Cabin that Sinatra began to hone his singing style, which soon began to attract attention. ("I think the song he sang most beautifully at that time was 'Begin the Beguine,' " Nancy would later note.) As Sinatra recalls, "We used to be on the air on a thing called 'The WNEW Dance Parade' in New York. They'd pick up little roadhouses and nightclubs, and we had fifteen minutes on the air every night, five nights a week. And that, of course, was very important to me, because people were beginning to hear me."

Musicians and entertainers heard him on the air or heard about him through word of mouth. They began to frequent the place, and, in later years, several of them would take credit for "discovering" Sinatra. Their stories would in fact form the prologue of assorted Sinatra legends later set in print. To this day, Sinatra still hears the tales.

"I don't care where I go, somebody will walk up to me and say, 'Gee, I was there the night that so-and-so came in and heard you, and...' Well, the club the man would be telling me about would be wrong. The city would be wrong. And the man he was talking about would be wrong. The only guy who came in and gave me a job was Mr. James."

"Mr. James" was, of course, Harry James. Only four months older than Sinatra, James had become a star of the Benny Goodman band in just two years, appearing weekly as a soloist on Goodman's network radio show. His trumpet playing was so acclaimed that he began to make plans to break away to form a band of his own— Harry James and the Music Makers, he planned to call it.

In those days virtually all network radio programs were broadcast twice, first for the East Coast, and then, three hours later, for the West Coast. Sinatra recalls that, while riding a band bus on a

*T*he Harry James band on the boardwalk in Atlantic City in 1939. James is seated in the center of the front row between his two vocalists, Connie Haines and Frank Sinatra ☆

series of one-nighters for James later that year, a band member told him how he came to James' attention.

"He explained to me that when they were all with Benny Goodman, they did a [radio] show at nine o'clock in New York and then another one at midnight for the [West] Coast. And between shows they would sit around in one of the hotel rooms and listen to the radio.... And they heard me on that program. And he told me that Harry said one night, 'If we ever get the band going...that's the kid, whoever he is, I want him to sing with the band.' And I was thrilled when he told me the story."

James set out on his own in February 1939. He was quickly booked for appearances at the Roseland Ballroom and at the Paramount in Times Square, New York's premier venues for big bands back then. And just before his first show he paid a visit to the New Jersey roadhouse where Sinatra was working.

"He came into the Rustic Cabin," Sinatra remembers, "and said he was starting a new orchestra, that he had left Benny Goodman's band, and he was looking for a boy singer."

James told Sinatra he couldn't offer him much money to sing with his band, just $75 a week. Sinatra grabbed the job. After all, he now had responsibilities: he had just married Nancy Barbato.

The wedding had taken place in Jersey City in a church Nancy's father had helped to build. She wore a white satin bridal gown and carried a white moiré taffeta prayer book, a gift from her

"Sinatra Joins James Ork"

The night after Sinatra met with Harry James at the Rustic Cabin, he found himself at New York's Roseland, Broadway's premier ballroom, standing in front of the James band for the first time, clutching a microphone and showing little sign of nervousness. In fact, members of the band would later recall that Sinatra radiated an enthusiasm and a charm that captivated them as much as it did the audience.

His name appeared in *Billboard* for the first time in July under the heading "Frank Sinatra Joins James Ork as Singer." The item read: "Frank Sinatra, cousin of maestro Ray, this week joined Harry James at the Roseland Ballroom, New York as vocalist. Young Sinatra is a Hoboken boy."

But in those days, crowds weren't drawn to venues like Roseland by the singers. Nor were critics. They rarely mentioned Sinatra or the band's female singer, Connie Haines, in their reviews. Sinatra, in fact, might as well have been a piccolo player—or a music stand, for that matter—for all the attention he got. Everyone knew that lyrics had been written for Harry James' swing hit "You Made Me Love You," but it would have been unthinkable for one of the band's vocalists to actually sing them. Harry James was the star of the band, and it would not be unusual for Sinatra to wait two or three minutes into a number, well past James' solo, before he would be called upon to render the lyric.

So Sinatra began acting as his own public-relations representative. He would collar critics, urging them to give him a write-up. He would harangue them with boastful predictions about his imminent fame.

And he began attracting fans. His voice was now heard on records; "From the Bottom of My Heart" and "Melancholy Mood" were originally recorded by the James orchestra as demos, with an announcer intoning on the first, "And now, in the language of swing, Harry phrases a bit of musical rhythm. 'From the Bottom of My Heart,' Frank Sinatra vocalizing." This song was later released on Brunswick Records. Sinatra's first official recording with the James

With an unidentified admirer in the early days.

husband-to-be, on which the florist had fashioned a wedding bouquet with lilies of the valley. Nancy later recalled, "As I started walking down the aisle on my father's arm...I started to cry. My dad was alarmed. He whispered in my ear, 'Is anything the matter?' 'Yes,' I said, 'I am so happy it's like pain.' I remember Frank's face as I walked down the aisle. He wasn't singing, of course, but...*he was*."

band was "All or Nothing at All." The label credited "Harry James and His Orchestra" and, in smaller letters, "Vocal Chorus, Frank Sinatra." It sold about eight thousand copies. (When it was rereleased in 1943, just after Sinatra had become a national sensation, the same recording became a runaway hit—but now Sinatra got top billing). The first records were not big hits, but they did get played on the radio, and they attracted the kind of attention Sinatra was seeking. When James' band left the Paramount and went on the road, Sinatra predicted his forthcoming celebrity status to anyone who would listen, and seemed as unbelievably bold and confident as Babe Ruth pointing to the spot where he would hit a home run.

Connie Haines once told Broadway columnist Earl Wilson, "The first theater we played on the road with James was the Hippodrome in Baltimore. Already the kids were hanging around the stage door, screaming for Frank. People said those kids were 'plants.' Plants! That's ridiculous. Who could afford to pay plants? Harry James couldn't afford to pay plants either. The band was having trouble financially, and we all hoped it wouldn't break up."

When the band reached the West Coast, it almost did. They were booked to perform in a swank, stodgy bistro in Hollywood called the Victor Hugo. It was the kind of place where waiters took care not to clink their serving utensils on the plates as they dished out pâté de foie gras. Guy Lombardo might have been well received there; Harry James was not. Four years later, when Sinatra and James reunited for a performance in Hollywood, gossip columnist Louella Parsons noticed that the two of them laughed and cut up during a performance of "All or Nothing at All." She asked Sinatra about what was clearly an inside joke between him and James. In her column in *Photoplay* magazine, she quoted Sinatra as saying:

"'All or Nothing at All' is the song that gave Harry and me our walking papers out of the old Victor Hugo cafe and, incidentally, out of Hollywood a few years ago, Louella. It was just four years ago this month that we were thrown out—right in the middle of that song. They didn't even let us get through it! The manager came up and waved his hands for us to stop. He said Harry's trumpet playing was too loud for the joint. He said my singing was just plain lousy. He said the two of us couldn't draw flies as an attraction."

The owner refused to pay the band. Nancy Sinatra had quit her job as a secretary at American Type Founders to be with her husband on the road. She was also pregnant. The debacle at Victor Hugo's left virtually every member of the band broke. Nancy later wrote, "It was really pretty frightening. There were two days there where we had nothing to eat but onion sandwiches.... I heard [Frank] say one day, and hope and pray I never hear such desperation in his voice again, 'My wife has got to eat.'"

As they headed back East, it seemed as if the band would no longer be able to stick it out. Sinatra didn't hang around long enough to find out.

In a playful mood with Marty, who worked by day as a fireman☆

The First Taste of Stardom

Opposite: Sinatra in one of his first Hollywood publicity photos, on the set of RKO's Higher and Higher. *The studio's caption said in part: "Actually, though, Frank Sinatra didn't know they were there." Left: By 1943, Sinatra was able to pack the* Hollywood Bowl, one of the country's largest venues at the time and a place where stars and studio magnates gathered in box seats behind a reflecting pool in front of the stage.

Tommy and Frankie

Below: With Tommy Dorsey in the studio.

Right: With Dorsey (left), Jo Stafford, and the Pied Pipers.

Frank soon learned that Tommy Dorsey was looking for a boy vocalist to replace Jack Leonard, probably the most famous band singer of the day, who was leaving the band to launch a solo career. Dorsey, Sinatra recognized, spotlighted his singers, even backed them up with an inventive and talented quartet called the Pied Pipers. "I wanted to sing with Dorsey more than anything else," he

said later. He went to James and asked to be released from his contract. "And Harry was very gracious," Sinatra says. "I had a two-year contract with him, and he just tore up the contract, and I went over with Tommy."

Dorsey also attracted some of the most gifted instrumentalists in the business, including Bunny Berigan, Pee Wee Erwin, Ziggy Elman, Charlie Spivak, Buddy De Franco, Bud Freeman, Joe Bushkin, Buddy Rich, and Louis Bellson.

EARLY ON, DRUMMER BUDDY RICH WAS KNOWN TO TAUNT SINATRA BY PLAYING LOUD DRUM RIFFS DURING HIS VOCALS; THIS PRACTICE ENDED THE SAME NIGHT RICH SHOWED UP ON THE BANDSTAND SPORTING A FAT LIP AND A MOUSE.

By temperament, Dorsey was about as passionate and unpredictable as his music, and some would later say that much of Dorsey's volatile personality rubbed off on Sinatra. Unquestionably, his musicianship did. "I learned about dynamics and phrasing and style from the way he played his horn," Sinatra said later. "Tommy Dorsey was a real education to me...in music, in business, in every possible way."

In fact, Sinatra's first recording with Dorsey, "I'll Never Smile Again," sounds, in mood, tone, and phrasing, remarkably like Dorsey's theme song and his biggest hit: "I'm Getting Sentimental Over You," which was written by a Canadian woman, Ruth Lowe, a former pianist in Ina Ray Hutton's all-girl band. She had left the band to marry Harold Cohen, a Chicago music publisher who died during an operation just a few weeks after their marriage.

Sinatra seemed to turn the meaning of Lowe's song on its ear. In his hands, it was no longer about eternal devotion. It was about unrequited love:

I'll never smile again
Until I smile at you
I'll never laugh again
What good would it do?

In June 1940, when Bob Hope went off the air for his annual vacation, the Dorsey band was hired to headline the summer replacement for his radio show. Lowe's song—and its singer—received nationwide exposure on that show. Within a few weeks, on July 20, 1940, *Billboard* magazine featured "I'll Never Smile Again" at number one on its very first chart of hit records.

Dorsey had paid Sinatra twenty-five dollars to record it. Singers did not receive royalties back then. And band singers were virtually nonentities. "In Tommy's band there were six singers [including the Pied Pipers]," Sinatra remembers, "and we just sat there [on stage] most of the time. And hardly anybody even knew our names."

But almost anyone who knew Sinatra then has described him as a brash, ambitious, likable kid determined to break out from the background of big band singing. In the June 1940 issue of *Swing* magazine it was reported that "Frank Sinatra is doing a pretty quick job of winning over Tommy Dorsey's fans and making new ones for himself. Like his novel idea of asking all those who request his picture to send theirs in return. (Must have an interesting collection!) Poised and friendly in appearance, which links strongly with a very capable voice.... Proudly displays a wedding band and boasts of the Mrs. and an expected addition to the family in June. Lad's full of pipe dreams with a collection of over 30—not dreams, pipes! Nice guy, Sinatra!"

Another newspaper item back then referred to Sinatra as "the romantic young baritone with the voice that thrills millions."

And Sinatra himself will concede that as he sat there on Dorsey's bandstand, waiting to sing an occasional song, he dreamed more than a few "pipe dreams."

"I guess I did. I don't think I thought much about it, but I had designs on one day breaking away."

And that recording of "I'll Never Smile Again" became the down payment on his ticket out of the band. "When we made 'I'll Never Smile Again,' then suddenly, the Pied Pipers and myself became household words in the country."

Sinatra soon found himself deluged with fan mail and requests for photographs. He (or Nancy, writing for him and copying his signature) took pains to respond to every letter. Magazines and newspapers were now publishing feature articles about him. He was no longer an anonymous band singer.

With Tommy Dorsey in 1956 for a "reunion" concert at the Paramount Theater. Dorsey died three months later.

A T THE CREST OF POPULAR ENTHUSIASM FOR "I'LL NEVER SMILE AGAIN," SINATRA BECAME A FATHER. NANCY SANDRA—FOR WHOM SINATRA'S CLOSE FRIEND, THE COMEDIAN PHIL SILVERS, WOULD EVENTUALLY WRITE THE SONG "NANCY WITH THE LAUGHING FACE"—WAS BORN ON JUNE 8, 1940, WHILE SINATRA WAS PERFORMING WITH THE DORSEY BAND AT THE HOTEL ASTOR IN NEW YORK. HE HAD TALKED TO HIS WIFE SHORTLY BEFORE THE SHOW, AND SHE HAD REMARKED, "DON'T BE SURPRISED IF IT DOESN'T HAPPEN TONIGHT." IN FACT, SHE HAD FELT CERTAIN THAT IT WAS GOING TO HAPPEN THAT NIGHT BUT FIGURED THAT HER HUSBAND WOULD EITHER NOT BE ABLE TO SING IF HE HAD HIS WIFE'S CONDITION ON HIS MIND OR—MORE LIKELY—THAT HE WOULD SKIP OUT ON HIS PERFORMANCE IN ORDER TO BE WITH HER. "I WOULDN'T LET THEM CALL FRANK AND TELL HIM [THAT I WAS IN LABOR]," NANCY LATER WROTE. "I DO TRY TO KEEP FROM HIM THINGS THAT I KNOW WILL DISTURB HIM."

To be sure, not all the press notices about him were complimentary. Most, in fact, were not. *Metronome* magazine grumbled, "He is not an impressive singer when he lets out—that's a cinch." But Tommy Dorsey recordings with Frank Sinatra vocals were becoming hot sellers: "The One I Love Belongs to Somebody Else," "Whispering," "The Night We Called It a Day," and "Night and Day" all sold well. At first Dorsey saw to it that his singer was not even mentioned on the record label, which credited "Tommy Dorsey Orchestra with Vocal Chorus." Sinatra threatened to go on strike unless he received personal credit on the records, and Dorsey finally relented.

Reports of the tiffs between Dorsey and Sinatra began to show up in the gossip columns. And Dorsey's friendly bandstand expression sometimes turned to frost as he watched couples halt their dancing and gather near the stage where Sinatra was singing. It also didn't help that Sinatra was regularly boasting in interviews that he was becoming more popular than Dorsey.

Says Sinatra: "Eventually the time did come when I said to Tommy, 'I'd like to try it on my own.' And I left the band and started out on my own. I didn't know where I was going, didn't have an agent or anything else. And I just started to book my own dates."

It was not a simple, friendly parting like the one with Harry James. Dorsey negotiated a contract termination—"a ratty piece of paper," Sinatra would later call it—that gave Dorsey one third of Sinatra's future earnings (for *life*). It would take the later efforts of several powerful agents and lawyers—and, according to Sinatra, $75,000—to persuade Dorsey to release Sinatra from his deal.

What might have been more worrisome for Sinatra at the time was that, although he recorded some ninety songs with the Dorsey band, no one was running after him now to offer work. He ended up back in New Jersey, performing at the Mosque Theater in Newark.

Golleee! You girls came here to see me? Pictures with adoring fans were almost always posed and often as goofy as this one.

But things were different now. Without Dorsey's restraining hand, Sinatra began playing to the teenage bobby-soxers in the crowds, turning them on with flirting eyes and quivering lips and vocal tricks that included sliding notes into a kind of guttural dip. And they began packing the halls. Eventually, Bob Weitman, manager of the Paramount, heard about Sinatra's allure and decided to drop by the Newark theater to see the young crooner. He was impressed.

The Day "All Hell Broke Loose"

The story goes that Weitman had a New Year's show, starring Benny Goodman, set to open on December 30, 1942. He went to Goodman and asked if he had any objection to adding Sinatra as a "special added attraction." Goodman reportedly replied, "Who the hell is

JACK BENNY TOLD NANCY SINATRA JR. ABOUT HER FATHER: "I INTRODUCED FRANK SINATRA AS IF HE WERE ONE OF MY CLOSEST FRIENDS—YOU KNOW I MADE A BIG THING OF IT AND I HAD TO MAKE ALL OF THIS UP, 'CAUSE I DIDN'T KNOW WHO HE WAS—AND THEN I SAID, 'WELL, ANYWAY, LADIES AND GENTLE-MEN, HERE HE IS, FRANK SINATRA'—AND I THOUGHT THE GOD-DAMNED BUILDING WAS GOING TO CAVE IN. I NEVER HEARD SUCH A COMMOTION. ☆"

Two unanswered questions: Whose eyes were bluer? and What would it have been like to sing "Love in Bloom" accompanied by Jack Benny on the violin?

Frank Sinatra?" Weitman got the same puzzled reaction when he asked Jack Benny to introduce Sinatra. But as Sinatra himself recalls the moment of his introduction that night: "I went into the Paramount, and all hell broke loose when that happened, and that was the beginning of it.... That's when the dam really broke, when I went in there by myself."

The audience response was indeed incredible. When Goodman, who had gone backstage, heard the screams of the teenagers who greeted Sinatra at the Paramount, he reportedly exclaimed, "What the hell was that?" Weitman later remarked, "I thought, you should excuse the expression, his pants had fallen down."

The press was cynical about the response that first night. A report appeared that a girl in the twelfth row who had waited in line all day without eating suddenly swooned from exhaustion when Sinatra walked on stage. A girl next to her screamed, and pandemonium ensued. But to Sinatra, who touched off the same, unbridled commotion night after night, the story seems dubious.

"I don't know about that," he says. "I mean the kids were squealing and yelling all the time. I don't even know how they could hear me, as a matter of fact. I don't know how they knew I could even sing, because there was so much noise going on."

To be sure, some of it—at least in the beginning—may have been instigated by press agent George Evans, who reportedly paid five dollars to teenagers to start screaming on cue. (Evans once offered to pay a thousand dollars to anyone who could prove he had used stooges; no one ever collected.) But after a short while, it became clear that the teenagers needed no prompting. Sinatra's most fanatic fans—the press called them "Sinatrics"—would gather by the hundreds around the stage door of the theaters and night-clubs where he was performing, the crowd surging around him and trying to touch him when he came out. The more brazen ones would try to tear off his clothes; once a middle-aged woman tore off her

own blouse and demanded that he autograph her bra. He began having to lay elaborate strategies to escape, exiting down fire escapes and barricading himself inside nearby shops. He once told of a time when he was caught between two girls who grabbed the two ends of his bow tie, nearly strangling him in the process.

Within months, no one in the country could rival Sinatra's popularity. Sinatra had been booked into the Paramount again on October 12, 1943, Columbus Day, a school holiday. And before dawn, the kids began to pack the subways and buses heading to Times Square. By afternoon, tens of thousands of them had gathered. Word went out that there was potential for a riot. It would be impossible for all the kids to get into the theater. An army of more than eight hundred police officers and police reserves was assembled outside the Paramount. By the time Sinatra appeared on stage for the first show, police estimated that forty thousand teenagers had jammed Times Square.

And what was it like for Sinatra to be at the center of this vortex? How was he affected by all that adoration? Well, he says he saw it mainly as a boost to his career. "I figured to myself, 'I guess I've got a shot at something here if it continues.' And it did continue."

None of the mini-riots, none of the hysteria seemed to faze Sinatra one whit. Everywhere he went, he would hear the screams—outside the theaters, outside his hotel rooms, outside the restaurants where he ate. He'd hear the shouts, "Frankie, I love you!" "Frankie, ohhhhhh, Frankie!" But never, it seems, did any of it

BEFORE SINATRA, POPULAR SINGERS GENERALLY DRESSED IN FORMAL GARB, LISTLESSLY DELIVERED ROMANTIC BALLADS, AND RECEIVED A POLITE PATTER OF APPLAUSE IN RESPONSE. THEY WERE TRAINED IN DELIVERY AND DICTION, IN VOCAL CONTROL AND TECHNIQUE. JO STAFFORD, A MEMBER OF THE PIED PIPERS WHEN SINATRA WAS SINGING WITH DORSEY, ONCE TOLD POP MUSIC CHRONICLER GEORGE T. SIMON: "WHEN I WAS WITH TOMMY DORSEY'S BAND MY SOUND WAS PERFECT—BUT BORING, TOO. THE NOTES MEANT MORE TO ME THAN THE WORDS. BUT THAT'S THE WAY I HAD BEEN TRAINED." SINATRA STRUCK GOLD WHEN HE WENT AFTER THE WORDS, INFUSING THE LYRICS WITH HIGH EMOTION—AND CREATING MASS HYSTERIA IN THE PROCESS.✫

become bothersome for him. Never once did he complain publicly about his fans, insisting that they were all "nice kids."

"No, it didn't annoy me, not in the least. I think I was just contented that everything was happening for me. I was just happy and went right along with it."

Sinatra's career exploded like a fireworks spectacle. Thousands of fan clubs were organized throughout the country—throughout the world—with names like The Society for Souls Suffering from

*Opposite, left: This 1943 RKO publicity photo highlighted the innocent, boy-next-door looks that aroused the maternal instincts— and the libido—of young women at a time when, as the song went, "what's good is in the army. What's left will never find me." **Opposite, right:** "Sinatrics" at the Paramount Theater, 1943. Some of these fans stood in three-deep lines that stretched around the block, returning day after day. **Left:** In a 1943 rehearsal for Your Hit Parade, Sinatra displays a signature end-of-song fillip.✫*

"The Voice"

The Frank Sinatra Show, sponsored by Lever Bros., debuted from Hollywood on CBS in January 1944. It was broadcast Wednesday evenings from CBS's largest audience studio on Vine Street (now the James Doolittle Theater). *Radio Life* magazine reported that Sinatra's fans would camp outside the theater beginning at 6:45 in the morning, bringing picnic baskets, scrap books of Sinatrabilia, and their adoration.

This program was a variety show—later renamed *Songs by Sinatra*—whose guest list included many of Hollywood's top entertainers. Often the show looked like a Dorsey band reunion, with the Pied Pipers providing backing vocals for Sinatra, Dorsey arranger Axel Stordahl conducting the music, and even Dorsey himself making guest appearances. But it was Sinatra whom the audiences came to see, and whom millions tuned in to hear. The show remained on the air, in one form or another, on one network or another, for fourteen years.

Sinatra's singing style began to evolve—on its own, it would seem. As he progressed from roadhouse singer to band singer to solo singer, he settled into his own style and honed his talents as a vocalist.

"I was trying to develop a style of singing that nobody else had, and I think it began to work."

Above: Reading the newspaper during a 1944 rehearsal. Right: Protected by a wall of police at his first West Coast appearance, 1943.

Sinatritis. Adults began packing some of New York's most fashionable nightclubs to see him. The American Tobacco Company hired him in February 1943 to host *The Lucky Strike Hit Parade,* giving him a chance to sing not only his own hit songs on the radio, but also everyone else's. *Life* put him on its cover. RKO signed him to a movie contract. By the end of 1943, he was reportedly earning a million dollars a year.

"I just kept on working and getting better all the time. I hoped I was getting better all the time anyway."

Sinatra described his style: "Well, it's called bel canto, in the Italian term about vocalizing. It means that you stay on a higher plain with your notes, rather than get them throaty. You make them pure, as pure as you possibly can make them."

If Frank had one continuing, underlying influence in creating his style, it was Tommy Dorsey. Dorsey's control was awe inspiring. He would play his trombone in such a way that he appeared only to be exhaling. When Frank Sinatra joined his band, he was amazed by Dorsey's control, and he endeavored to do vocally what Dorsey was doing instrumentally: sing a dozen bars or so without breathing, to keep the music flowing. "I worked on that all the time," he says. "And I worked on things physically, exercises and swimming and stuff, and that helped a great deal."

"I tried to sing in the fashion that Tommy was playing the trombone, where he would play twelve measures without seeming to breathe."

When writers for music publications interviewed him, the same question would always come up. "Whenever they began to discuss my style of singing," Sinatra says, "they'd always say to me, 'Well, when do you breathe?' And I'd say, 'That's a big secret. I can't tell you that.'"

It is a singing style that you don't often hear on Sinatra's more recent recordings or performances. "I can't practice that technique as well anymore," he says, "because when I was younger, it was easier to do. My muscles were all brand new. But I still work at it, and I think it works. I still try to do that."

NYPD's finest—male and female—mobilizing for the expected throng at the Paramount Theater in 1944.

W̶ith Lana Turner in Hollywood in 1944. By this time, Sinatra's look of sweet innocence was beginning to fade.

Critics began to write reams of panegyric copy about the music that Sinatra was creating. Even jazz critics would join the debate, although to this day many insist that Sinatra was always one hundred percent pop. No singer has won *Downbeat* magazine's readers' poll more often than Frank Sinatra. In fact, in one survey for the *Encyclopedia of Jazz* Musicians' Musicians poll, Sinatra was placed at the top of the list. However, the late jazz critic Leonard Feather, who edited the encyclopedia, observed, "My own feeling is that…Frank Sinatra, though certainly the jazzman's favorite singer, is not a jazz artist."

There have been a good number of music critics who have written that Sinatra did things with his voice that no white singer before him had ever done. But when Sinatra is asked today about that appraisal, he chafes a bit and responds, "I don't know what that means. I really don't."

But while Bing Crosby once acknowledged that his greatest influence was a black vaudevillian named John Bubbles (a star of the Ziegfeld Follies and later, of Hollywood), Sinatra only allows, "John Bubbles I got to know later on. And John Bubbles was a very good jazz singer, and I used to listen to him a great deal. And I listened to Louie Armstrong, …Billie Holiday, and Mabel Mercer…. I really studied their singing, and I thought, 'I should be able to get something from all of them.' And I did. They influenced me here and there."

Sinatra's musical progression is evident on his early recordings. His style seemed to undergo a subtle change from one record to the next. Study photographs of Sinatra, and you can almost match the maturing voice with the maturing features on his face.

Sinatra's lifestyle, however, was undergoing change that was anything but subtle. The pauper had been transformed practically overnight into the king. And he luxuriated in his riches. Gossip columnists linked him with film stars Lana Turner and Marilyn Maxwell. They said he was so loaded that he passed out $150 gold cigarette lighters to friends as trinkets. He wore expensive monogrammed shirts and tailored suits with shoulder pads bigger than a zoot suit's.

But the one thing that he wanted to earn more than anything else—respect—seemed to elude him. In California, he was booked to sing with the Hollywood Bowl Symphony Orchestra. The Bowl was packed with teenage girls who screamed while their boyfriends jeered, and the critics didn't know what to make of it all.

When Sinatra was booked at the Lewisohn Stadium in New York as a soloist with the New York Philharmonic, the *Herald-Tribune*'s critic, Paul Bowles, said that his performance was "more revealing sociologically than from a musical standpoint…. He sang harmless Tin Pan Alley tunes to a chorus of hysterical feminine voices synchronizing their screams as he closes his eyes and moves his body sideways."

Society columnist Elsa Maxwell sniffed that the screamers ought to be given "Sinatraceptives." And indeed, it seemed as if the women in his audience were making love to him from their seats.

When Sinatra's first movie for RKO, *Higher and Higher*, was released, *New York Times* film critic Bosley Crowther sneered that it ought to have been called *Lower and Lower*.

Moreover, there was a war going on. GIs figured that girls in America should be finding their heroes among those in uniform. They resented the skinny guy who pulled a 4-F classification because of an ear disorder but who seemed as physically sound as any of them. Sinatra never joined any of the USO (United Service Organizations) entertainment tours in Europe during the war, probably because he realized that it was likely he would be received as warmly as a German S.S. officer.

In time, Sinatra grew weary of the noise that attended all his public performances. And so did his radio audiences. Old Gold cigarettes, the sponsor of *Songs by Sinatra*, began receiving complaints that Sinatra's singing could not be heard because of all the din from studio audiences.

Sinatra decided to take matters into his own hands. Just before going on the air for his West Coast broadcast one night, he stepped in front of the curtains at the radio studio and asked his audience to calm down. The noise, he said, made it impossible for people at

Leaving the Army Induction Center in Newark, New Jersey, in December 1943. Sinatra was classified 4-F because of a punctured eardrum.

Apparently mistaking Sinatra for his golf bag, Bob Hope prepares to tee off with Bing Crosby at a celebrity golf tournament in 1944.

SINATRA'S PRESS AGENTS WERE ABLE TO CONVERT HIS PHYSICAL LIMITATIONS INTO ASSETS. TAKE THIS DIALOGUE FROM A BOB HOPE RADIO SHOW IN MAY 1947, FOR EXAMPLE, WHERE SINATRA PLAYS ALONG:

HOPE: WHAT ELSE HAVE YOU BEEN DOING, FRANK?

SINATRA: WELL, I HAD A TOUGH BREAK THE OTHER NIGHT, BOB. I WAS A GUEST ON *THE RED SKELTON SHOW*, AND YOU KNOW THE COMMERCIAL THAT GOES *WHOOOOOSH*?

HOPE: YEAH, WHAT ABOUT IT?

SINATRA: WELL, THE SOUNDMAN WORKED IT BACKWARDS BY MISTAKE. SUCKED ME RIGHT BACK INTO THE MICROPHONE.

HOPE: DON'T KID ME, FRANK. YOU LOOK SKINNY, BUT YOU'RE PLENTY RUGGED. HOW DO YOU DO IT?

SINATRA: WELL, YOU SEE, BOB, I EAT RAW MEAT.

HOPE: WHO LIFTS IT FOR YOU? UH, I MEAN, WHERE DO YOU GET RAW MEAT?

SINATRA: I TAKE IT AWAY FROM LEO THE LION AT METRO GOLDWYN MAYER.

HOPE: HE PROBABLY THINKS YOU'RE THE WHIP!☆

home to hear his songs; it spoiled the show. The tactic didn't work. The screaming started up again on the very first number. He tried again when the audience for the East Coast broadcast arrived, this time telling the crowd that they would no longer be invited back if they continued screaming. The audience ignored his plea. "No more audiences," Sinatra said when it was over. And for the next several weeks *Songs by Sinatra* was performed in front of empty seats.

His audiences got the message. They were eventually invited back—and they behaved.

Continuing to grasp for respect, Sinatra began to explore classical music, becoming a collector of hundreds of classical albums. He cultivated friendly relationships with opera singers, symphony conductors, and eminent soloists. He sought them out and eagerly discussed music theory and technique with them—even though he himself could not read a note of music. The language of music was universal, he determined. He convinced himself that what he was doing for a living was not all that different from what, say, violinist Jascha Heifetz was doing.

"I heard some records of Heifetz, and I thought, 'He has a flow with the bow across the strings so that nothing was perceptible when he broke the phrase—you couldn't hear it. When he bowed up and then reversed and came down, there was just that infinitesimal break,' and I thought, 'If I could do that vocally, it would be more different than what I'm doing now,' and I started to work on that, and that worked for me too."

In 1945, Sinatra told the American composer Alec Wilder that he wanted to conduct some of Wilder's works with a symphony orchestra for a Columbia Records album. The result earned Sinatra praise not only from Wilder but from several established classical music critics who had previously regarded him as just a pop music phenomenon.

In those days, hundreds of articles tried to explain Sinatra's appeal. Most of what was written was strictly psycho-nonsense. He was frail, appealing to the motherly instincts of girls, some articles said. He looked like a teenager himself, as if he were one of them. He may not have had the classical good looks of matinee idols, but there were those mesmerizing blue eyes.

Sinatra himself had few illusions about why he had been singled out for collective passion. "Psychologists tried to go into the reasons with all sorts of deep theories," he once said. "I could have told them why. Perfectly simple; it was the war years and there was a great loneliness, and I was the boy in every corner drug-store, the

WHEN SINATRA MADE HIS FIRST TRIP TO HIS ANCESTRAL HOMELAND, ITALY, IT WAS AFTER V-E DAY (MAY 8, 1945, THE DAY MARKING THE GERMAN SURRENDER TO ALLIED FORCES IN WORLD WAR II) AS PART OF A USO TOUR. BUT HE CUT THE TRIP SHORT BECAUSE OF THE OVERWHELMING NEGATIVE REPORTS OF HIS PARTICIPATION IN THE TOUR. (A *STARS AND STRIPES* EDITORIAL HOOTED, "MICE MAKE WOMEN FAINT, TOO.") YET COMEDIAN PHIL SILVERS, WHO APPEARED WITH SINATRA ON THAT TOUR, WROTE IN A LETTER TO THE *HOLLYWOOD REPORTER* FROM ITALY, "[SINATRA] IS THE BIGGEST SENSATION THE USO EVER HAD. HE'S THE MOST COOPERATIVE, REGULAR KID YOU'VE EVER SEEN. EVERY CAMP WE'VE BEEN TO—HE WAS GREETED BY DERISIVE SCREAMS FROM THE MEN BECAUSE OF HIS SWOONING PUBLICITY. BUT WHEN WE LEAVE, THEY LOVE HIM TO A MAN.... THE SHOW WAS PLANNED WITH THAT IN MIND. I USE HIM AS A STOOGE, SLAP HIM AROUND FOR MOST OF THE SHOW—AND THEN, WHEN HE SINGS, THE GUYS ARE REALLY READY FOR HIM."

Signing autographs and posing for photographs for servicemen during a USO tour in Italy at the end of World War II. The GIs would be going home soon, and Sinatra would no longer be their rival

while others dismissed them. The verse, he believed, was essential to the drama, the buildup of a song. Every woman who listened to him could easily convince herself that he was carefully wooing her, that the music was an element of foreplay. Men, too, could become overwhelmed listening to him sing about a love gone wrong.

"I get an audience involved, personally involved in a song," said Sinatra in a 1963 *Playboy* interview, "because I'm involved myself.... When I sing I believe I'm honest."

His entrances were also part of the act. Unlike other performers, who would enter from behind the bandstand, Sinatra would enter from the back of the room, letting everyone in the audience see him up close and even make eye contact with him.

boy who'd gone off drafted to the war. That's all.... Forget all this nonsense about everyone wanting to 'mother' me."

What was generally overlooked in all the attempts to assess Sinatra's charisma was that he was a superb actor, that he could convey the angst of a popular lyric with a power and skill shared by only a few today—Barbra Streisand and Tony Bennett, for instance. It was the reason he continued to sing the verses of songs

"That's America to Me"

In 1944, at a time when the entertainment industry was solidly Republican, Sinatra risked alienating his colleagues and millions of Republican fans by expressing his admiration and support for Franklin Roosevelt and making a hefty contribution to the Democratic party. The president invited him to the White House and asked him how he was able to make women swoon. Sinatra replied that he wished he knew.

Conservative columnists laid into him after his White House tête-à-tête. He became the whipping boy of the Hearst newspapers' chief Roosevelt baiter, Westbrook Pegler. Sinatra himself abruptly became a political issue. George Chatfield, the New York state commissioner of education, publicly threatened to have him arrested for contributing to juvenile delinquency and truancy. "We cannot tolerate young people making a public display of losing control of their emotions," he said.

"Well, he was probably running for reelection," Sinatra says when reminded of those kinds of diatribes. "Anybody who would make that kind of statement—I mean, that really borders on the ridiculous. That was silly. I mean, we weren't contributing to any delinquency. I couldn't keep tabs on every single youngster who wanted to come and hear me sing, but I don't think too much bad happened in those days with those kids. They were better then than they are now."

But it was true that Sinatra was becoming an intense advocate of social causes. He made a permanent mark in one early film, a "short subject" devoted to the theme of tolerance called *The House I Live In*, for which he received a special Oscar in 1945.

Perhaps because of his unthreatening slightness, perhaps because he looked almost like one of them, Sinatra formed a special bond with young boys. He put this bond to good use in the film The House I Live In, *which addressed the issue of racial intolerance*

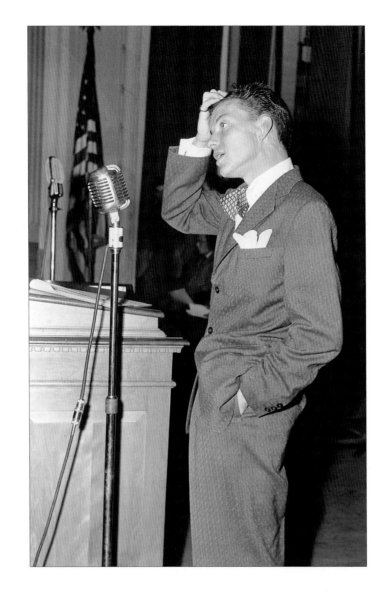

Shortly before he made *The House I Live In*, he visited a high school in Gary, Indiana, where white students had walked out to protest the principal's efforts to integrate the school orchestra and swimming pool. He delivered a stirring talk to the students and accused some of the local politicians of attempting to foment the trouble. He recalled that when he was in high school, he had often had ethnic epithets hurled at him. He closed by endorsing "the American way" and asking the kids to join him in singing the national anthem.

In reviewing *The House I Live In*, *Time* magazine commented, "This well-meaning project...part of a larger Sinatra crusade...was staged with free help from topflight Hollywood talent. They got the idea for the picture when they learned that Sinatra had been making spontaneous visits to high schools where he preached little sermons on tolerance."

Cue magazine commented succinctly: "Sinatra takes his popularity seriously. More. He attempts to do something constructive with it."

In fact, he received an entire trophy case full of awards for his work in that film. One of them came from an organization called American Youth for Democracy, which would later be identified as a communist front organization by California's Un-American Activities Committee, chaired by state Senator Jack Tenney. The committee, in taking note of the award to Sinatra, observed that American Youth for Democracy was actually an outgrowth of the Young Communist League and that it "follows the Communist Party line assiduously."

The following year Sinatra became a vice chairman of The Hollywood Independent Citizens Committee of the Arts, Sciences and Professions. Its members included such other vocal and liberal-leaning personalities as Humphrey Bogart, Charles Boyer, George Burns, Abe Burrows, Eddie Cantor, Joseph Cotten, Olivia de Havilland, Joan Fontaine, John Garfield, Ira Gershwin, Paulette Goddard, Rita Hayworth, John Houseman, Walter Huston, George Jessel, Jerome Kern, Jesse Lasky, Gregory Peck, Edward G. Robinson, Artur Rubinstein, Artie Shaw, Walter Wanger, and Orson Welles. The group was branded a communist front by the Tenney committee, which in 1948 placed Sinatra's name near the top of a long list of its more notorious critics. "These persons are typical of

THE LEAST VISIBLE MEMBERS OF THE ENTERTAINMENT INDUSTRY—WRITERS, DIRECTORS, EVEN STAGEHANDS—WERE THE ONES WHOSE CAREERS WERE MOST LIKELY TO BE EXTINGUISHED BY THE BLACKLISTERS. A FAMOUS NAME GAVE SOME PROTECTION FROM ATTACK. WHEN COMMENTATOR WALTER WINCHELL REVEALED THAT LUCILLE BALL HAD ONCE BEEN A MEMBER OF THE COMMUNIST PARTY, SHE WAS ALREADY THE MOST POPULAR WOMAN IN AMERICA. HER EXPLANATION THAT SHE HAD JOINED TO PLEASE A DEMANDING, RADICAL GRANDFATHER WAS QUICKLY ACCEPTED BY HER FANS, WHO ALL LOVED LUCY AND DOUBTED SHE COULD EVER BE INVOLVED IN A CONSPIRACY TO OVERTHROW THE GOVERNMENT. SHE LATER ACKNOWLEDGED THAT SHE WAS "LUCKY" TO HAVE ESCAPED OSTRACISM AND LAMENTED THE FACT THAT MANY OF HER FRIENDS DURING THAT PERIOD HAD NOT☆

*I*N 1955 SINATRA AND PLAYWRIGHT ARTHUR MILLER FORMED A COMPANY, COMBINED ARTISTS, TO MAKE A MOVIE IN WHICH SINATRA WOULD STAR AS A SOCIAL WORKER FROM NEW YORK CITY'S YOUTH BOARD. TO RESEARCH HIS STORY, MILLER HAD ACCOMPANIED ACTUAL YOUTH BOARD WORKERS ON THEIR ROUNDS OF BROOKLYN, WHERE TWO RIVAL GANGS, THE VICEROYS AND THE DRAGONS, WERE DECIMATING ONE ANOTHER IN A SERIES OF REVENGE KILLINGS. MILLER SUBMITTED A TWENTY-NINE-PAGE TREATMENT OF HIS FILM TO THE CITY'S BOARD OF ESTIMATES, WHICH APPROVED A CONTRACT.

BUT CONSERVATIVE COLUMNISTS POUNCED ON THE DEAL, CHARGING MILLER AND SINATRA WITH "FELLOW TRAVELING" (ASSOCIATING WITH COMMUNISTS), AND THE YOUTH BOARD WITHDREW ITS COOPERATION. MILLER RESPONDED, "THE MAJORITY OF THE YOUTH BOARD HAS NOW DECIDED THAT THIS PICTURE SHALL NOT BE MADE. SO BE IT. NOW LET'S SEE WHETHER FANATICISM CAN DO WHAT IT NEVER COULD DO IN THE HISTORY OF THE WORLD: LET IT PERFORM A CREATIVE ACT. LET IT TAKE ITS CLUB IN HAND AND WRITE WHAT IT HAS JUST DESTROYED."

the individuals within the various Stalinist orbits, about whose activities in Stalinist programs and causes your committee has presented factual reports or has taken sworn evidence," the Tenney committee said in a report to the California legislature.

It was a time of the blacklist, when film producers feared that their movies might be boycotted if they hired left-wing actors, directors, or writers who, the public suspected, might sneak "un-American" propaganda into their films or use their earnings to support causes aimed at "overthrowing the government." It was a time when television producers feared they would lose advertisers if it was revealed that a communist or "fellow traveler" was associated with their programs.

In the late 1940s, when left-wing filmmakers were charged with contempt of Congress for refusing to testify before the House Un-American Activities Committee investigating communist influence in Hollywood, Sinatra was one of the few to sign an amicus curiae brief on their behalf. (Albert Maltz, a member of the infamous Hollywood Ten, imprisoned for contempt of Congress, wrote the screenplay for *The House I Live In.*)

"Once they get the movies throttled," Sinatra declared at the time, "how long will it be before the committee goes to work on freedom of the air? How long will it be before we're told what we can say and cannot say into a radio microphone? If you make a pitch on a nationwide radio network for a square deal for the underdog, will they call you a commie?... Are they going to scare us into silence? I wonder."

The chairman of the House Un-American Activities Committee, J. Parnell Thomas, responded by calling Sinatra "a sort of a Mrs. Roosevelt in pants."

None of the political attacks deterred Sinatra. He invited Eleanor Roosevelt, who was anathema to conservatives, to appear on his television show in 1955 to recite the words to his hit song

Sinatra remained a steadfast friend to Eleanor Roosevelt even when she was arguably the most controversial woman in America.

Sinatra chats with a reporter while ignoring Lee Mortimer, standing behind him at Beverly Hills Justice Court in April 1947.

"High Hopes." In the late 1950s, he was one of the first to announce his willingness to hire a blacklisted writer. He became a friend and confidant of John Kennedy, contributing to the young senator's campaign for the presidency. He recorded a special version of "High Hopes" as a campaign song for Kennedy and became one of his leading fund-raisers. By now he was in the thick of things, politically, and he would maintain a passionate commitment to politics throughout his career.

The Mob Connection

His fame and political involvements made him a lightning rod for criticism on many fronts. Over time his patience with the antagonistic press ran out.

While there were certain standards that Hollywood journalists adhered to—they never attacked performers who were just establishing a name for themselves, they never mentioned an established actor's alcohol or drug addiction, they never discussed affairs overtly (though they would drop broad hints), and they never even approached the issue of homosexuality—there was still plenty of room for gossip and for feeding the fantasies of a public that idolized their favorite stars. The *New York Post*'s Sydney Skolsky, for example, offered a weekly celebrity profile—he called it a "tintype"—that concluded with a description of what kind of bed the celebrity slept in and what he or she wore to bed, if anything. (Sinatra, for the record, slept in a double bed and wore light cotton pajamas, according to Skolsky.)

Many of these writers presented themselves as friends of the stars and reported their intimate contacts with them. If they were scorned by stars, they would often retaliate with the accumulated "power of the press." For the most part, Sinatra got along fine with the Hollywood columnists, but there was one altercation with the muckraking Lee Mortimer.

Few men have ever denigrated journalism as odiously as Mortimer. He spent a lifetime attempting to smear the reputations of celebrities, particularly those with a politically liberal bent. In the early forties, he wrote a sludgy gossip column in the old New York *Mirror*. He also wrote a series of exposé books of dubious authenticity with "confidential" in their title.

In April 1947 Mortimer wrote in the *Mirror* that Sinatra had become a buddy of the notorious gangster Lucky Luciano and had flown to Havana to deliver two million dollars in small bills to him. (The charge, like others that followed claiming that Sinatra engaged in illegal activities with mobsters, was never substantiated.)

Another columnist, Robert Ruark, had also been tipped off about Sinatra's encounter with Luciano. He wrote:

"Mr. Sinatra, the self-confessed savior of the country's small fry, by virtue of his lectures on clean living and love-thy-neighbor, his

movie shorts on tolerance, and his frequent dabbling into the do-good department of politics, seems to be setting a most peculiar example for his hordes of pimply, shrieking slaves, who are alleged to regard him with the same awe as a practicing Mohammedan for the Prophet."

In fact, Sinatra had met Luciano in Havana, but *his* story was that this happened when he was invited to have dinner at a casino with a number of notables one night. One of the casino hosts recognized him and asked if he would mind meeting a few special guests, one of whom turned out to be Luciano. "I was brought up to shake a man's hand when I am introduced to him, without investigating his past," is the way that Sinatra described the encounter. Later that night, he ran into Luciano again, who invited him and a friend to join him at his table. "Rather than cause a disturbance," Sinatra said, "I had a quick drink and excused myself. Those were the only times I have ever seen Luciano in my life."

Later, in a letter to columnist Hedda Hopper, he insisted that when he shook hands with Luciano, "even if I'd caught his name, I probably wouldn't have associated it with the notorious underworld character. He was headlines before my time."

It now seems apparent that Mortimer, Ruark, and other writers of articles linking Sinatra to Luciano were part of a right-wing push to cut down outspoken show-business liberals. The same columnists who were now attacking him for associating with gangsters had previously attacked him for associating with communists. Every time he appeared at a fund-raising affair for an organization supporting liberal causes, he was damned for assisting a "communist front."

By the late 1940s, federal government intelligence agencies had become powerful, semi-autonomous outfits with little oversight. With World War II over, the American public were convinced that a war must be waged on crime and communism. The FBI's J. Edgar Hoover was quick to respond, becoming arguably Washing-ton's most notorious official, as much a household name as the president.

Hoover assigned staff members of the Federal Bureau of Investigation to work with radio producers to produce weekly programs devoted to the bureau's efforts to eradicate crooks and "commies." *Gangbusters, The FBI in Peace and War, I Was a Communist for the FBI*, and other shows presented the bureau's cause in the most patriotic terms and helped raise the "red scare" to fever pitch. An army of hack writers worked avidly for the FBI, knowing that Hoover, now with a vast network of wire-tapped phones at his disposal, could be the source of invaluable information for stories.

Ruark and Mortimer had almost certainly been tipped off by Hoover or an aide about Sinatra's brush with Lucky Luciano in Havana. But Sinatra did not see their published attacks as part of a political strategy aimed at liberals like himself. He saw them as a

A 1976 photograph of Sinatra with alleged members of the mob in his dressing room in Westchester, New York. At far left is Gregory De Palma. At right are (from left) Thomas Marslow, Carlo Gambino, and Jimmy "The Weasel" Fratiano. This photo would later haunt the successful crooner.

The Author Remembers

Salvatore Lucania, a.k.a. Charles "Lucky" Luciano. Lucky courted friendships with numerous celebrities.

SINATRA'S STORY IS NOT AT ALL DIFFICULT FOR ME TO ACCEPT. I HAD A SIMILAR ENCOUNTER WITH LUCIANO. IN 1961 NEW YORK THEATRICAL AGENT GEORGE WOOD—CALLED "THE VICE PRESIDENT FOR DEALING WITH THE MOB OF THE WILLIAM MORRIS AGENCY" BY THE LATE MAX AZNAS, OWNER OF MANHATTAN'S STAGE DELICATESSEN, AND IDENTIFIED BY KITTY KELLEY, IN HER BOOK ON SINATRA, AS HIS AGENT THERE—ARRANGED FOR ME TO MEET LUCIANO WHILE I WAS IN ITALY ON ASSIGNMENT FOR ABC-TV NEWS. LUCIANO, WOOD SAID, WAS WRITING HIS AUTOBIOGRAPHY, AND SOME ADVANCE PUBLICITY MIGHT STIMULATE INTEREST AMONG PUBLISHERS.

UPON ARRIVING IN ITALY, HOWEVER, I FOUND OUT THAT HE HAD LEFT HIS FLAT IN NAPLES, AND WAS TOLD THAT HE WAS SPENDING THE SUMMER WITH HIS BROTHER.

MIKE STERN, THE PUBLISHER OF THE ROME *AMERICAN*, TRACKED LUCIANO DOWN FOR ME IN SANTA MARINELLA, A SEASIDE TOWN SOME THIRTY MILES NORTHWEST OF ROME, WHERE HE WAS LIVING UNDER THE FAMILY NAME OF LUCANIA. IT SEEMED LUCIANO WANTED TO MEET BEFORE HE WOULD AGREE TO APPEAR ON CAMERA. THE NEXT DAY, I TOOK A TRAIN TO THE COAST AND WAS MET BY LUCIANO'S NEPHEW, WHO DROVE ME TO THE HOUSE—BARELY MORE THAN A SHACK—WHERE THE ONETIME GANGSTER WAS STAYING.

WE SAT ON A PATIO WHILE FIREFLIES BY THE MILLIONS BUZZED AROUND US, AND LUCIANO PLAYED THE AFFABLE HOST, AT ONE POINT WANDERING INTO THE KITCHEN AND RETURNING WITH A TRAY ON WHICH HE HAD PLACED BOTTLES OF SCOTCH, BOURBON, AND VODKA, ALL BEARING WOOLWORTH'S LABELS. "I DON'T DRINK," HE SAID, "BUT HELP YOURSELF TO ONE OF THESE."

HE TOLD ME THAT HIS LIFE HAD BEEN UTTERLY DISTORTED AND MYTHOLOGIZED BY THE PRESS, THAT HE WAS NEVER "AN ORGANIZED-CRIME KINGPIN" AS SOME IN THE UNITED STATES HAD CALLED HIM. HE HAD ONCE HAD A FEW "RACKETS," A FEW "GIRLS," HE SAID, BUT THAT WAS ALL.

BUT WHEN I ASKED HIM WHAT INFORMATION HE HAD GIVEN THE U.S. GOVERNMENT TO EARN HIS RELEASE FROM DANNEMORA PRISON IN NEW YORK AND HIS DEPORTATION TO ITALY AFTER THE WAR, HE CLAMMED UP. "THAT WILL BE IN THE BOOK," HE SAID.

"SUPPOSEDLY GOVERNOR DEWEY SIGNED ORDERS FOR YOU TO BE RELEASED AS A REWARD FOR GIVING AUTHORITIES INVALUABLE INSIDE INFORMATION ABOUT ITALIAN SABOTEURS WORKING ON THE NEW YORK WATERFRONT DURING THE WAR," I SAID. "WHO WERE THOSE SABOTEURS? WHAT WERE THEY PLANNING TO DO? AND WHAT HAPPENED TO THEM?" HE REFUSED TO ANSWER. BUT HE DID AGREE TO AN INTERVIEW, TO LAST NO MORE THAN TWENTY MINUTES, WHICH, WE ARRANGED, WOULD TAKE PLACE TWO DAYS LATER IN THE BACK OFFICE OF A RESTAURANT IN NAPLES THAT HE FREQUENTED. I DECIDED TO SAVE MY QUESTIONS FOR THEN.

"SAY," HE SAID, "I'M DRIVING INTO ROME TO GO TO THE TROTTING RACES. COME WITH ME, AND I'LL DROP YOU OFF AT YOUR HOTEL AFTERWARDS." I ACCEPTED THE INVITATION AND WE PILED INTO HIS BATTERED ALFA ROMEO, STOPPING ON THE WAY TO PICK UP A YOUNG LADY.

ITALIAN AUTHORITIES HAD ONLY RECENTLY LIFTED RESTRICTIONS ON LUCIANO'S MOVEMENTS IN ROME; HE HAD PREVIOUSLY NOT BEEN ALLOWED TO SET FOOT IN THE ITALIAN CAPITAL. ON OUR WAY TO THE RACETRACK, HE BECAME LOST—DIRECTLY IN FRONT OF ST. PETER'S BASILICA IN VATICAN CITY. HE STOPPED THE CAR AND APPROACHED TWO POLICE OFFICERS STANDING ON A CORNER, ASKING THEM FOR DIRECTIONS TO THE TROTTING RACES. AS HE THANKED THEM AND TURNED AWAY, ONE OF THE OFFICERS TURNED TO THE OTHER AND REMARKED ALOUD, "LUCKY LUCIANO." LUCIANO BEAMED PROUDLY.

"YOU SEE, LEW," HE SAID, "THEY RECOGNIZE ME!"

LUCIANO MADE RATHER SMALL WAGERS (I DID NOT GAMBLE AT ALL), AND I COULD NOT TELL WHETHER HE WAS WINNING OR LOSING. HE NEVER SEEMED TO SHOW MUCH REACTION TO THE OUTCOME OF A RACE. LUCIANO'S GIRLFRIEND SNAPPED PICTURE AFTER PICTURE OF THE TWO OF US SITTING SIDE BY SIDE IN THE STANDS, AND THE FLASHES OF HER CAMERA SOON ATTRACTED ATTENTION. OTHER PEOPLE BEGAN TAKING PICTURES OF US, TOO. AND IT OCCURRED TO ME, "WHAT IF ONE OF THESE PHOTOS SHOULD END UP BACK HOME IN SOME SCANDAL SHEET ABOVE A CAPTION LIKE, 'GANGSTER LUCIANO ENTERTAINS ABC REPORTER AT RACE TRACK'? OR WHAT IF THEY LANDED IN AN FBI FILE?"

TWO DAYS LATER I ARRIVED AT THE NAPLES RESTAURANT WITH A CAMERA CREW AT THE APPOINTED TIME FOR OUR INTERVIEW. LUCIANO DID NOT SHOW UP FOR MORE THAN AN HOUR. WHEN HE FINALLY ARRIVED, HE TOOK ME ASIDE AND TOLD ME THAT HE WOULD NOT APPEAR ON CAMERA UNLESS HE WAS PAID. THE MAN WHO HAD BEEN SO AFFABLE AND BUOYANT TWO DAYS EARLIER WAS NOW REMOTE AND ALOOF, ESPECIALLY NOW THAT HE KNEW SOMEONE WAS GOING TO CONSIDERABLE EXPENSE TO GET HIM IN FRONT OF A TELEVISION CAMERA.

THE INTERVIEW NEVER TOOK PLACE. LUCIANO DIED A FEW MONTHS LATER OF AN APPARENT HEART ATTACK AT A TRAIN STATION. AS FAR AS I AM AWARE, NO PART OF THE AUTOBIOGRAPHY HE SAID HE WAS WRITING AT THE TIME WE MET HAS EVER APPEARED IN PRINT, AND ONE CAN ONLY SPECULATE AS TO THE WHEREABOUTS OF THE MANUSCRIPT.

SELECT COMMITT
ON CRIME
PUBLIC HEARIN
Room 345

knock at him personally. What he did next, he did out of a sense of pride. He slugged Mortimer.

On April 8, 1947, at Ciro's, a nightclub on Hollywood's Sunset Strip, Sinatra spotted Mortimer sitting at a nearby table. The two exchanged unfriendly glances, and when Mortimer started out the door around midnight, Sinatra came after him and belted him behind the left ear. He also reportedly screamed at the columnist, "I'll kill you the next time I see you."

The attack drew no blood—but it caused plenty of ink to flow, especially after Mortimer had the singer arrested for assault and battery. After Sinatra pleaded not guilty, he was released on five hundred dollars' bail. Mortimer then threw a counterpunch—he sued Sinatra for twenty-five thousand dollars in damages.

At the time, Hollywood columnists were as mighty as the most despotic studio mogul. Newspaper readers often turned to Hedda Hopper, Louella Parsons, Walter Winchell, Erskine Johnson, or Sidney Skolsky before they even glanced at the rest of the news. Now a columnist had been physically assaulted by a celebrity he had written about...that they *all* had written about.

The damage-control patrol immediately shifted into high gear. Sinatra's publicists advised to telephone each columnist and explain that he had nursed a growing resentment over the despicable manner in which Mortimer continually referred to his fans. Still, he was to say, he had not planned to take a poke at Mortimer until the columnist walked past him and called him a "dago." Sinatra followed his publicists' advice.

Curiosity seekers

wait in line to attend

a July 18, 1972, House

Crime Committee

hearing concerning

Sinatra's alleged links

to the Mafia.

Signing autographs

with Hollywood gossip

columnist Louella

Parsons. Sinatra

polarized Hollywood

writers; while many

excoriated him, most

of the leading ones

stood by him ✩

Eventually, Mortimer accepted a settlement of the lawsuit, and Sinatra issued an apology, in which he stated that "on further inquiry" he had "ascertained" that Mortimer had made no racial epithet against him.

Still, Louis B. Mayer, the vice president and general manager of Metro Goldwyn Mayer (MGM), remained concerned. He feared that Mortimer and other columnists who were regularly published in the Hearst newspapers would continue to attack not only Sinatra personally but the movies he was making for the studio. Since Mayer had long ago formed an alliance with Hearst, whose news corporation still produced the "News of the Day" newsreels for MGM, the studio reportedly arranged a private meeting between Sinatra and William Randolph Hearst at Hearst's estate in Beverly Hills. Sinatra, it was said, pleaded his case well. It also helped, it seems, that Marion Davies, Hearst's longtime mistress and a former actress herself, attended the meeting. She apparently adored Sinatra and despised Mortimer. Hearst reportedly issued orders to his writers to lay off Sinatra.

In any event, knowledge that Sinatra was prepared to use his fists to defend his honor did not deter other writers over the years from linking him with underworld hoods. Sinatra has never denied that he has associated with gangsters. But, he has always been quick to add, so has every other major entertainer in this country. Underworld figures have dabbled in show business since the days of Prohibition speakeasies, and entertainers with Italian surnames have been particular favorites. A publishing empire could be founded on books about Hollywood celebrities with ties to gangsters.

Kitty Kelley's 1986 biography of Sinatra attempted to document Sinatra's mob associations in lurid detail; she produced depositions and government documents obtained through the Freedom of Information Act substantiating that Sinatra had numerous contacts with known organized-crime figures. But she was unable to produce, the slightest bit of evidence that Sinatra had ever engaged in any illegal conduct on behalf of or in association with those crooks.

He may, as has been charged, have accepted favors from them, may even have invested in some of their legitimate businesses, like hotels, casinos, and nightclubs. But he also *worked* in those places. Surely no one wants to disappoint his employer—especially if his employer happens to be a mobster.

Indeed, Sinatra has been investigated meticulously. He has been compelled to testify in front of grand juries and congressional committees and has been questioned by police authorities on every level of government.

Former Los Angeles County Sheriff Peter Pitchess, in a letter to Nancy Jr., once recalled that he had been contacted by Nevada investigators who were looking into her father's alleged ties to organized crime.

"I told them, 'I have probably spent more time investigating Frank Sinatra than any other man or organization. First, because I was acting in the intelligence section of the FBI when I was an agent; then as sheriff; then because Mr. Sinatra is my personal friend and I had to find out to protect my career. And let me tell you something: You might just as well go home because you're not going to confirm any of those things.'"

Shortly after Sinatra was summoned to testify at a House subcommittee hearing on crime in 1972, *The New York Times* printed on its Op-Ed page an article written by him charging that such committees "can become star chambers in which 'facts' are confused with rumor, gossip and innuendo, and where reputations and character can be demolished in front of the largest possible audiences."

Frankie Goes to Hollywood

Frank Sinatra made his first film appearance in *Las Vegas Nights* with the Tommy Dorsey Band in March 1941. His first speaking part came in *Higher and Higher* for RKO in December 1943, in which he played, ironically enough, the "boy next door." Two hit records came out of those movies, "A Lovely Way to Spend an Evening" and "I Couldn't Sleep a Wink Last Night," both written by Jimmy McHugh and Harold Adamson.

His first starring role for RKO was in *Reveille with Beverly*, a film with a plot as silly as its title. But it featured Sinatra singing one of Cole Porter's most enduring compositions, "Night and Day," and it showed that Frankie could set off squeals from the screen as deftly as he could from the stage. It was quickly followed by *Step*

In his case, Sinatra observed, "a convicted murderer [Mafia enforcer Joseph Barboza] was allowed to throw my name around with abandon, while the TV cameras rolled on. His vicious little fantasy [Barboza testified that Sinatra had been used as a "business front" by a Mafia capo] was sent into millions of American homes, including my own. Sure, I was given a chance to refute it, but as we have all come to know, the accusation often remains longer in the public mind than the defense."

Sinatra went on to say that the public seems especially willing to accept gossip and speculation about stars and in his own case, he suggested, perhaps it is even more tractable, "because my name ends in a vowel." He insisted once again that people "want to believe that if an entertainer is introduced to someone in a night club, they become intimate friends forever." But, said Sinatra, once such "fantasies" are connected to "real, live human beings," those individuals "have to go on living with their friends, family, and business associates in the real world."

But the *New York Times* piece failed to silence the gossip mongers. And years later, Kelley's "unauthorized biography"—the most extensive rehash of the Sinatra/Mafia muck—became a bestseller.

*B*efore teaming
up with Gene Kelly,
Sinatra's idea of
performing was
limited to clutching
a microphone and
letting his lower
lip quiver during a
ballad. Kelly taught
him to use his
entire body while
performing☆

Sinatra wrote that Kelly "popped straight up like a champagne cork, did a mid-air somersault, came down in a leg-split, and segued into a tap routine that sounded like a nest of angry machine-guns. Suffice it to say, I was impressed."

Sinatra wisely accepted Kelly's offer to serve as dance instructor. He worked diligently with Kelly for eight weeks, at the end of which time, Sinatra joked, "I've got seven hundred torn ligaments, compound fractures in every bone in my body, and I've lost vitally needed weight." But he also received "the ultimate compliment" from Kelly:

"Francis, you've worked your way up from lousy to adequate. I'm ready to dance on camera with you."

But, it would seem, Kelly did more than just turn Sinatra into a dancer. He also taught him how to act, something that Sinatra himself would acknowledge at a Friars Club roast of Kelly in 1975:

"He had the patience of Job, and he had the fortitude not to punch me in the mouth because I was impatient.... It took a lot of time to do these things, and I couldn't understand why I took so much time. He just managed to calm me when it was important to calm me. We were doing something that we wanted to do. We loved doing it, and I loved it. He taught me everything I know. I couldn't walk, let alone dance. I was a guy who got up and hung onto a

*L*eft: Pupil and mentor: Frank Sinatra and Gene Kelly rehearsing a number for Anchors Aweigh. **Below:** Nancy Jr. getting special attention from dad at MGM's famed commissary in 1945. Seated in the background are costars Gene Kelly and Pamela Britton ☆

Lively, a musical version of the Marx Brothers' *Room Service,* and the film in which Sinatra received his first screen kisses, from Gloria de Haven and Anne Jeffreys.

Still, he was no actor. He looked embarrassingly awkward and stiff in those early RKO stabs at celluloid stardom. But Louis B. Mayer realized that Sinatra had great box office potential. He brought him to MGM and paired him with Gene Kelly on *Anchors Aweigh* (1945).

Sinatra, in a preface to Clive Hirschhorn's biography of Kelly, recalled his first meeting with the dancer-star.

"I've got a five-tube radio, so I know you can sing," Kelly remarked, according to Sinatra. "The important thing is, can you dance?"

Sinatra pointed to his feet and promised, "These here babies can do anything I tell 'em to do!"

"Good," said Kelly. "Tell 'em to do this!"

With young party-goer Eddie Hodges in A Hole in the Head *(1959), directed by Frank Capra. The film was produced by Sincap—a fusion of Sinatra and Capra.*

In 1949 Sinatra performed in his first straight acting role in The Miracle of the Bells. It was said that he was assigned the role of a Catholic priest to help restore his tarnished image after the brawl with Lee Mortimer and to boost his career, which by now was sliding further than Dorsey's trombone.

The strategy didn't work. "Frank Sinatra...acts properly humble or perhaps ashamed," said Time magazine. And James Agee said in his review, "I hereby declare myself the founding father of the Society for the Prevention of Cruelty to God."

The few bells that rang on box office cash registers tolled a death knell for the movie.

microphone with both arms together, and a bad tuxedo, and brown shoes. And all of a sudden I was a star. And one of the reasons why I became a star was Gene Kelly."

Anchors Aweigh became one of the few musicals ever to be nominated for a best-picture Oscar.

In 1949 Sinatra made two more films with Kelly: *On the Town* and *Take Me Out to the Ball Game. On the Town* probably represented Sinatra's top performance in a musical, but it didn't draw the crowds it would have attracted only a few years earlier, during the Swoonatra hysteria.

Although he was holding his own in Hollywood, he realized that the kind of movies he was being called upon to perform in were as disposable as chewing gum. MGM never even bothered to change the flavor. Sinatra once remarked: "In *Anchors* I was cast as a friendly little sailor with nothing much to say for himself. Then came *It Happened in Brooklyn*, where I played the part of a friendly little GI with nothing much to say for himself. By the time we reach *On the Town*, they'd made me a sailor again, as inarticulate as ever.... You see the rut I was in! Even the story was mostly the

same. Gene Kelly and Sinatra meet girl, Kelly hates girl, Sinatra loves girl, girl likes Sinatra but loves Kelly, girl rejects Sinatra, Sinatra finds that he loved another girl all the time, Kelly finds out that he loved the first girl all the time—fade out. Sometimes it was someone else instead of Gene, but any other variations were strictly superficial."

Sinatra's impatience with the filmmaking process earned him the reputation of being "difficult." Sitting around in a dressing room waiting to be called for a scene that might last a few seconds was not Sinatra's idea of what stars were supposed to do. He had no patience for the process of filming take after take of the same scene. And he found lip-synching in movies to his own prerecorded voice especially constraining, noting that, to this day, he never sings a song the same way twice.

It wasn't until Frank Capra directed Sinatra in *A Hole in the Head* in 1959 that anyone figured out how to make the most of Sinatra's talents. As Capra later wrote: "I noticed that his best

These days singers may spend days—weeks even—laying down the vocal track for a single song on an album. Sinatra would often record an entire album in less than three hours, often with time to spare.

performance came on his first take. As takes continued, he would never reach that first show of brilliance. The other actors were just the opposite, even such an old pro as Edward G. Robinson. They all improved with each take. I devised a simple way of overcoming this. I just had someone else do Sinatra's lines until the other actors had the scene down pat. Then I called Frank. He's a performer first, actor second. That's why his first shot is always the best."

The same could have been said of Bing Crosby, and in fact Sinatra and Crosby—both of whom had reputations for being difficult on the set—worked remarkably well together. In *High Society* (1956), they performed some of the most difficult scenes in one take and gave the musical numbers a sense of spontaneity and enthusiasm that might have been lost if they had been forced to conform to conventional filmmaking procedures.

Another director who came to terms with Sinatra's aversion to rehearsals and retakes was Otto Preminger. In his autobiography

Yes, I Can!, Sammy Davis Jr., recalled that he accompanied Sinatra to the studio when he was making *The Man with the Golden Arm* (1955) for Preminger. The director had allotted an entire week to shoot a scene in which Sinatra undergoes the rigors of heroin withdrawal. But, wrote Davis, "Frank got there on the very first morning and said, 'Come on, Ludwig [Sinatra's nickname for Preminger]. Get the cameras rolling. I know exactly how this thing's got to be played. Forget the rehearsals.' Preminger risked it, and it became a classic scene, one of Sinatra's finest pieces of acting."

Frank's ride in Hollywood was bumpy, though, even when the reviews were good. There was the trouble the press had in accepting his politics. And there was the trouble the public had watching Frank's fairy-tale family life ruined by his capricious romantic entanglements.

Left: Artist Saul Bass' remarkable poster for The Man with the Golden Arm *(1956).* **Above:** *With an ever-so-laid-back Bing Crosby during a 1948 radio show* ☆

LOVE AND MARRIAGE

(and Divorce)

*O**pposite:** Returning to New York from Hollywood in 1943. Even the presence of the two Nancys, who showed up to greet him, did not dampen the enthusiasm of Sinatra's followers. According to one news report of the day, shortly after this picture was taken, nine "frantic female fans" fought their way through police and bodyguards and ripped the buttons from his suit. **Left:** Frank and Ava's relationship was the most tempestuous courtship, marriage, and divorce in Hollywood history. Songs might have been written about it. And Sinatra might have recorded them all ☆*

The Picture Cracks

The photographers get photographed— along with Nancy and newborn Frank Jr.

During the height of Sinatramania, it was clear that the public loved the whole package—Frank the performer, Frank the family man. In the popular imagination, the Boy Next Door had been married to the Girl Next Door. Nancy Sinatra had told stories about fixing spaghetti for her husband and the Dorsey band when they were all struggling.

When Frank Jr. was born, someone had arranged for a throng of photographers to snap her in her hospital bed, holding the baby, with a picture of her husband in her lap. Most of the press photos of the Sinatras together presented them greeting one another after Frank's return from some out-of-town performance.

"Nobody comes before my wife, Nancy," he had said when Sinatramania had first erupted. "That goes for now and for all time."

In the beginning there was hardly a girl in America who didn't envy Nancy. Over time, however, as Frank's infidelities became public, it became clear there was little to be envious about.

Few friends of the couple dared to come to Nancy's defense. Instead, they conspired to set Sinatra back on the right track every time he strayed. On one memorable evening, comedian Phil Silvers invited Nancy to the opening night of his show at Slapsie Maxie's nightclub. He did not tell her, however, that her wayward husband had been invited to perform that night as well. But suddenly, there was Frank, singing—as corny as it may seem—a song called "Going Home." When he finished, Silvers led him over to where Nancy was sitting. Nancy and Frank hugged, and the audience gave them a standing ovation.

Such episodes were common. Frank Sinatra had not become a star in order to surrender the right to live as he wished.

One person who did confront Sinatra was columnist Hedda Hopper—a "tough old dame," he once called her. At an awards party staged for Sinatra at the Hollywood nightclub Ciro's by *Modern Screen* magazine, Hedda collared him. As she later described the incident in her column:

"He was surprised. He didn't say anything. I did all the talking, and it was straight from my heart.

"'Look, Frank,' I told him. 'It's none of my business—but I think you're making the mistake of your life! I've never been a red hot booster of yours, but I admire you and how you've handled your career, up till now. But I'm an older woman and I want to tell you something for what it's worth to you.' I let him have it....

"I sat down and talked to him like a Dutch aunt. I told him what a wonderful career he'd had, what a wonderful one lay ahead, but I warned him that he was public property now and that part of that public property was Nancy and his children....

"When I was through, Frankie said, 'Hedda, no one ever talked like that to me before.'

"I'm sure no one had. He'd heard nothing but 'yesses' and raves for four years. He'd turned tone-deaf to criticism. He was hungry for frank, honest opinion.

"'Look,' suggested Frank, 'I want to talk some more. Can you have lunch with me next week?' I said I certainly could. Well, we didn't have that lunch because Frank and Nancy were back together again before then. But what struck me about the whole thing was Frank's reaction to a good bawling out. He could have snapped, 'Mind your own business!' and I'd have been put right in my place.

"I was speaking without caginess, saying what I thought. Frank appreciated it. What's more, he didn't sulk or nurse a grudge. On the contrary, when Frank and Nancy and all their friends staged

their wonderful New Year's Eve party—for my money the greatest private show ever put on in Hollywood—I was the only newspaper reporter in town invited. And I appreciated that."

But finally the same whirlwind of success that produced uncountable riches for Sinatra landed him in the arms of some of the most glamorous women in Hollywood. He was first linked to Lana Turner and Marilyn Maxwell, two stunningly alluring women. Sinatra soon discovered that any number of not-so-famous but equally glamorous Hollywood wanna-bes were easy scores. When his indiscretions became public, his fans were bewildered.

Typical of this bewilderment was this letter sent to Hedda Hopper dated October 13, 1946:

"We have a terrible let-down feeling to find our idol has feet of clay. We have felt all along that Frankie and his family were sort of our special property. And after reading in all the screen and radio magazines about his family life and how devoted he was to [his wife and kids], now it just all seems like, as our parents tell us, just Hollywood publicity.

"I have been going to write you ever since Frank Sinatra walked out on Nancy. I used to listen to him because I thought he was different from the rest of that trash in Hollywood. But now I am burned up. Lana Turner must be proud of herself to break up a nice

With columnist Hedda Hopper, wearing one of her outlandish hats, on the set of Some Came Running *(1959)*.

Eckstine, Frankie Laine, Bing Crosby, and Mel Tormé. In January 1950, Evans died of a heart attack. In February, Nancy announced their separation. In May, Frank was dropped from *Your Hit Parade.* His records stopped selling. He had even become estranged from his father and mother.

And then Louis B. Mayer got word while he was in the hospital recovering from a fall off a horse that Sinatra had made a joke in public about Mayer's relationship with the singer Ginny Simms. ("He didn't fall off a horse, he fell off Ginny Simms," Sinatra had said on the set.)

As Sinatra described the consequences in his daughter Nancy's biography, *Frank Sinatra, My Father,* Mayer called him into his office after his recovery and said, "So? I hear you been making jokes about my lady friend."

"Yeah, oh, I wish I could take that back. I'm so sorry. I wish I'd *never* said anything so stupid."

"That's not a very nice thing to do. I want you to leave here, and I don't ever want you to come back again."

Almost immediately, MGM began negotiations with Sinatra's agent at MCA to buy out his movie contract for $85,000. When Nancy heard about the deal, she persuaded a judge to instruct the studio to pay the money directly to her as interim support. Sinatra began receiving frequent phone calls from his children, who would ask him again and again when he was coming home; these calls often reduced him to tears.

He was forced to cancel all nightclub dates after experiencing what has been variously called "a massive throat hemorrhage" or "hysterical aphonia" on stage at the Copacabana nightclub in New York on May 2, 1950. Skitch Henderson, who was leading the orchestra that night, later wrote that this incident occurred during the third and final show of that evening.

"He opened his mouth to sing after the band introduction and nothing came out! Not a sound! I thought for a fleeting moment that the unexpected pantomime was a joke. But then he caught my eye. I guess the color drained out of my face as I saw the panic in his. It became so quiet in the club—they were like watching a man walk off a cliff. His face chalk white, Frank gasped something that sounded like 'Good Night' and raced off the floor, leaving the audience stunned. It was tragic and terrifying."

The Copa engagement was canceled. Sinatra headed to Tossa del Mar on the Mediterranean to recuperate. Not coincidentally, Ava Gardner was vacationing there as well.

Sinatra has always been close to his kids. Today Frank Sinatra Jr. is his father's musical director ☆

little family like the Sinatras. The public should boycott all the pictures of girls like her. [Her affair with Frankie] is a fine example to set for the younger people."

At first, his press agent, George Evans, kept a tight lid on dormant scandals and tried to persuade his client to keep his natural urges under control. But by 1949, it wasn't hard to conclude that Sinatra's bubble was about to burst. He had dropped from number one in *Downbeat's* annual poll to number five, behind Billy

A scene of model domesticity: Dad arriving home from work bearing gifts for the kids; Mom, wearing a fashionable apron over a fashionable dress, about to set dinner on the table. So what was the photographer doing in the house?

At home with the two Nancys, little Tina, and Frank Jr. Even after the marriage to Nancy ended, she and Frankie remained friends. Neither she nor any of their children ever uttered an unkind word about him publicly.

Without Evans, Sinatra's infidelities became a full-blown public scandal. Reporters swooped around him like vultures. Photographers lay in wait for him, hoping to snap his picture arm in arm with some new "other woman."

When confronted by reporters about the behavior of her husband, Nancy took a he-always-comes-back stance—and at first he did. After one separation, when he closed a radio broadcast by saying, "Good night, Nancy," the audience broke into wild cheering.

But when Sinatra began his peripatetic pursuit of Ava Gardner in 1950—and didn't come back—Nancy filed for divorce.

O NCE, WHEN ASKED ABOUT HIS ALLEGED PHILANDERING BY MEMBERS OF THE PRESS, SINATRA REPLIED, "I CAN HONESTLY SAY THAT IF I HAD AS MANY LOVE AFFAIRS AS YOU HAVE GIVEN ME CREDIT FOR, I WOULD NOW BE SPEAKING TO YOU FROM A JAR IN THE HARVARD MEDICAL SCHOOL ☆ "

Ava

Sinatra's affair with Ava Gardner may have begun even before he met her. It was said that his was a case of love at first sight and that the "first sight" came when he spotted her in the pages of a movie magazine while he was still singing with the Dorsey band and told a musician that this was the woman he would marry one day.

In her autobiography, written just before her death in 1990, Gardner said that she first met Sinatra when she was still married to Mickey Rooney. "'Hey, why didn't I meet you before Mickey?' Gardner recalled Sinatra saying. "'Then I could have married you myself.'"

In the beginning, their affair was carefully shielded from the press by their own press agents. Movie stars were required by the "morals clauses" in their studio contracts to present themselves to the public as chaste, wholesome icons. These were the days when the most shocking word uttered on the screen was Clark Gable's "damn" in *Gone with the Wind*, when even actors playing man and wife were required to sleep in separate beds. But these were also the days when gossip columnists made their reputations revealing how often and in how many ways those moral codes were broken. So there were careful measures taken to keep indiscretions private. Moreover, Sinatra was a Catholic, and the church viewed infidelity and divorce in those days with the same degree of opposition as it did (and does) abortion.

Ava Gardner had already been married twice (to Rooney and bandleader Artie Shaw) when she began seeing in 1949. At the time, he was still carrying on an affair with her friend, Lana Turner. Sinatra and Gardner were under contract to MGM, a studio ruled with an iron fist by Louis B. Mayer. Mayer was determined to impose moral standards on the performers who worked for him, and he regarded the gossip about Sinatra and Gardner as an embarrassment to his studio. When Gardner came to him one day in 1950 to ask his permission to leave the studio to attend Sinatra's opening of the Shamrock Hotel in Houston, he said no. When she persisted, he unleashed a barrage of invectives at the woman who had become one of MGM's most alluring stars. When she left his office, she got in her car and drove to the airport, taking the first plane to Houston. She later told biographer Roland Flamini that she thought at the

Despite all the gossip about his womanizing, Sinatra almost always appeared to be enjoying marital bliss. A trip out of town? A publicity photographer was on hand to capture Nancy helping him pack ☆

At times, Ava and Frank appeared to be mirror images of one another: the high cheekbones, the flaring eyebrows, the toothy smiles. They were also very much alike beneath the skin☆

time, "Neither Metro nor the newspapers nor anyone else is going to run my life."

The reporters were waiting for her in Houston, and they dogged her and Sinatra everywhere. One night in Houston, while they dined at an Italian restaurant as guests of Mayor Oscar Holcombe, Edward Schisser, a photographer for the *Houston Post*, approached their table and asked to take a picture. Sinatra later said he politely declined. Schisser claimed Sinatra's exact words were, "Beat it, you bum." Schisser refused to move. When it looked as if Schisser was going to snap the picture anyway, Sinatra leaped to his feet and was about to punch the photographer when Ava Gardner screamed and covered her face. Sinatra sat down and the photographer left. The event was duly reported.

Through it all, Ava Gardner maintained a friendship with her second husband, Artie Shaw, often asking him for advice. She would later recall a conversation with her ex that went like this:

GARDNER: He wants to marry me.

SHAW: What about you? Do you want to marry him?

GARDNER: I've got to.

SHAW: What do you mean, you've got to?

GARDNER: How would it look if I didn't? I pulled him away from Nancy. Now he's having a tough time.... I've just got to, that's all.

What Gardner could not understand was why she had to continue her romance with the singer secretively, why Sinatra simply couldn't get a divorce and be done with it. And although Sinatra reportedly assured her he was "working" on a divorce for more than a year, stories repeatedly appeared in the press about how he had patched things up with Nancy.

It was an affair to be remembered through Sinatra's music at the time: "No One Cares," "In the Wee Small Hours," "It's a Blue World," "I'm a Fool to Want You." The songs would all serve as a fitting soundtrack if a movie about the Sinatra-Gardner romance was ever made☆

Meanwhile, the romance was followed like a daily soap opera in the Hollywood columns. Hardly a week went by without some new juicy bit of gossip being leaked about the ups and downs of the affair. In her autobiography, Gardner wrote: "I didn't understand then and frankly, I still don't understand now why there should be this prurient mass hysteria about a male and female climbing into bed and doing what comes naturally. It's blessed in weddings, celebrated in honeymoons, but out of wedlock it's condemned as the worst of sins. Maybe people are paying too much attention to the 'lock' part of wedlock. And maybe, just maybe, there's a touch of jealousy somewhere."

In April 1950, when news of the romance had become common knowledge, Sinatra wrote a rather cryptic letter to columnist Hedda Hopper.

"Dear Hedda,

"Now that the sound and the fury have died down a little, I embark on a small voyage of thanks. It has been a great temptation to write you sooner but, after all, you are a newspaper woman and you do have a living to make and the last thing I would want to do is

*S*he was the embodiment of Hollywood allure, a top box office attraction. He was a fast-fading singer. What did she see in him? The gossip columnists wanted to know ☆

make you think I was asking you to lay off. Now that my situation is no longer the hot news it seemed to be, I want you to know that I have never experienced an evidence of greater friendliness and that I shall never forget it. Your kindness in the face of the multitude of embarrassing truths and the even greater number of untruths that were printed and spoken on the radio, will forever overwhelm me.

"Believe me, Hedda, they had me digging pretty deep below the surface—and then I had the great good fortune to strike the gold of your friendship.

"Gratefully,

"(s) Frankie"

Hopper later wrote: "I could recall no specific incident that inspired the letter."

But the columnists never let up their criticism of the affair. Hedda Hopper was now regularly reproaching Sinatra in print. In

October she received a phone call from him. As she later reported in her column, he told her, "You could be wrong."

"Certainly I can. Anybody can be wrong," Hopper said she replied. "But, Frank, I can think of nobody who can be as wrong as you. You have Nancy and the children to consider; also thousands of fans who love you and your family. If you really love Ava, why don't you get a divorce and marry her? A divorce would at least make your affair legitimate and get the press and public off your neck. Right now, you're being unfair to both Ava and Nancy. Many think that after you've had your fling with Ava, you'll return to your family. That's a humiliating position for both girls."

In April 1950, Ava was working in Spain making *Pandora and the Flying Dutchman.* European gossip writers—who were even less reliable than their American counterparts—reported that Ava was dating a handsome Spanish bullfighter, Mario Cabre, who was appearing in the movie, and quoted Cabre as saying that he loved Ava "with all the strength in my soul" and that he believed she loved him. He even wrote her poems ("idiotic," Gardner would later call them). When Cabre was asked about a diamond necklace that Sinatra had reportedly sent to Ava, he reportedly replied, "Well, symbolically, that would be like giving her a noose...trying to hang love...trying to rope her in!"

It seems, however, that it was actually Cabre who was trying to rope her in. "Mario got carried away confusing his onstage and off-stage roles," Gardner wrote in her autobiography. "In every country in the world, you find men who are pains in the ass. Mario was a Spanish pain in the ass, better at self-promotion than either bull-fighting or love."

But Gardner, "after one one of those romantic, star-filled, dance-filled, booze-filled Spanish nights," did wind up in bed with Cabre, and Cabre now wanted to spread the news to the world.

Cabre publicly warned Sinatra that if he wanted to try to take her away from him, he would not leave Spain alive. When Sinatra heard the threat, he took the next plane to Madrid.

There, he confronted Gardner about the press reports, and she responded that she and Cabre were "just friends." Cabre was nowhere around (the director had whisked him away to a shoot in Gerona, many miles away). Gardner and Sinatra spent the next two days holed up in Tossa del Mar. Sinatra left Spain a few days later, blaming the Spanish press for spreading "vicious gossip" about Ava. When Sinatra arrived in New York, a reporter asked him whether he had run away from the bullfighter.

"No, I didn't run away from him, and, no, he didn't cramp my style. They're working in a picture together and that's all there is to it." As for Cabre's remarks, Sinatra called them "a publicity stunt."

When filming of *Pandora and the Flying Dutchman* wrapped up in July, Ava and Frank took off for a vacation together in Mexico. But the press again was hounding them, and as they attempted to change planes in El Paso, Sinatra shouted to the writers, "This is silly.... What we do is our own damn business.... It's really a fine thing when we can't even go on vacation without being chased."

On November 1, 1951, Sinatra's divorce from Nancy became final. The next day, he and Ava Gardner applied for a marriage license in Philadelphia. On November 7, in Germantown, Pennsylvania, they were married.

If opposites attract, what is there to say about duplicates?

It is difficult to envision two more kindred characters than Frank Sinatra and Ava Gardner. They were both from humble begin-nings and ended up becoming icons of their time. They were both

Bottom left: Leaving a Las Vegas courtroom after being granted a divorce from Nancy. Both had filed for divorce—Frank in Vegas and Nancy in Santa Monica—and each had stated "mental cruelty" as grounds.
Left: *Sinatra and Gardner's marriage-license application. He gave his occupation as "entertainer"; she listed hers as "actress."*

The traditional wedding photo: holding hands behind the wedding cake. This picture was perhaps the only thing about Frank and Ava's marriage that could be called "traditional."

exceedingly conscious of their shortcomings and did their damnedest to surmount them. Both indulged an overabundance of the seven deadly sins (with jealousy taking the place of sloth). They were hard-core, two-fisted drinkers. They could, when enraged, condense every adjective in the English language to four letters beginning with "f". They perceived relationships with others as fundamentally competitive. Both required love and devotion in greater abundance than either was capable of giving. They were charismatic personalities who were deluged with love and devotion from throngs of anonymous admirers. They were fiercely possessive of each other. And both perceived existence as an exhilarating adventure.

Their clashes all seemed to relate to these identical attributes. But even though their relationship often seemed to be a clash of the titans, Frank and Ava were small fry compared to the genuine titans who sought to exert control over them. For both, there was MGM potentate Louis B. Mayer. For Gardner, there was Howard Hughes.

Hughes was a man determined to get what he wanted—and he usually got it. Ava Gardner, however, was the exception. Prior to her relationship with Sinatra, Gardner had dated Hughes and he had lavished her with jewelry. But, she always insisted, they had never slept together. Not that Hughes hadn't wanted to. She simply rebuffed him each time he made advances.

But Hughes refused to give up — even when Gardner's affair with Sinatra became front-page news. Intent on degrading Sinatra in Gardner's eyes, he hired a team of detectives to delve into Sinatra's past. The most incriminating evidence his private eyes could turn up was that Sinatra, while performing at the Copacabana in New York, had been carrying on an affair with a chorus girl in his show.

Ava and Frank walking hand in hand in the sand during their Miami Beach honeymoon. Wherever they went, photographers were never far behind.

Linked on the links in Las Vegas in 1953. By then, their marriage had become as erratic as his golf game.

In her autobiography, Ava Gardner seems to look back on her marriage to Frank Sinatra with a kind of rueful nostalgia. She depicts her raucous spats with him as if they were scenes out of an X-rated version of *I Love Lucy*, reducing all the quarrels that finally wrecked their marriage to simple absurdity.

For example, Gardner's description of herself trying to catch Sinatra in a compromising act with Lana Turner at his Palm Springs home is funnier than any comic sketch. After arriving at home and finding the drapes drawn over the front windows, Gardner began sneaking around the side, hoping to find a window that she could peek through. Just as she pressed her nose against the kitchen window, the back door flew open and she heard the voice of Lana Turner's manager, Ben Cole, who said, "Ava, is that you? Come on in, honey." Gardner called out to her mother, who was waiting in a car parked on the street, and they went in to the house. Turner was there with Cole, but Sinatra was not in attendance. It seems that Frank had lent the house to Turner and she was waiting for her current boyfriend to arrive from Los Angeles. The four of them then began having a party when the front door opened and Sinatra walked in.

"Ah, Frank! I thought you were going to be down here fucking Lana," Gardner said drunkenly.

SINATRA: I wouldn't touch that broad if you paid me.
TURNER: I'm leaving, I'm leaving.
SINATRA: Out of my house. Out, out, out! Everybody out!
GARDNER: Okay, but in my own time. Taking my books and records and personal belongings with me.

Sinatra concurred and began gathering up Gardner's belongings and tossing them out the front door. He was about to throw Gardner out too, but she held tightly onto a doorknob.

GARDNER'S MOTHER: For God's sake, kids. Will you please knock it off? This is *disgraceful!*
SINATRA: The police. I'm going to call the police.
GARDNER: Great idea. Call the police. Call the fucking police.

Cole then asked whether he could retrieve the cold chicken and drinks he and Turner had brought. In the meantime, a time-out occurred. A few minutes later, the police chief, who was a friend of Sinatra's, arrived, calmed everyone down, and left.

"As you might imagine," Gardner wrote in her biography, "it took Frank and me a little time to make up after that escapade."

Hughes phoned Gardner at Sinatra's home in Palm Springs and arranged to see her. He arrived with the detectives' documentation in hand: the name of the girl, her telephone number, the times and places she had met Sinatra—"the whole routine," as Gardner would later describe it. Although she said she confronted Sinatra and the girl about Hughes' evidence (they both denied that they had slept together), she decided to let the matter ride and told Hughes, "This kind of shit cuts no ice with me."

But then on the night before their wedding she received a handwritten note from an admitted prostitute who claimed that she, too, had been having an affair with Sinatra. She provided what Gardner would call "details that I found convincing"—so convincing, in fact, that Gardner decided to call the wedding off. It took an entire night of arguing with friends and Sinatra himself, according to Gardner, to persuade her to go ahead with it. Years later, Gardner said, she realized that the prostitute's letter had probably been instigated by Howard Hughes.

Both admitted to having short fuses. Gardner told columnist Sidney Skolsky in October 1953. "Honey, I've got to let off steam... Frankie and I are both high-strung people. We explode fast. Maybe faster than most married couples, but they all have hassles."

For his part, Frank followed Gardner onto sets—even if the sets were on another continent—jealous of anyone who commanded her attention. They continued fighting. Over anything. After one fight at a hotel, Sinatra pretended to shoot himself while talking to Gardner on the phone. After another, he took an overdose of sleeping pills.

There were frequent separations and frequent public reconciliations, including one during Adlai Stevenson's election campaign in October 1953. Ava introduced her husband at a campaign fund-raiser in Hollywood. "I can't do anything myself," she said, "but I can introduce a wonderful, wonderful man. I'm a great fan of his myself. Ladies and gentlemen, my husband, Frank Sinatra."

"Politics," commented columnist Earl Wilson, "makes strange...reconciliation."

Doing It His Way

For all the wild antics going on in the background, the quality of Sinatra's work was ever higher.

He appeared in fine form, relaxed and assured, and his voice seemed stronger than ever. Every so often, when he realized he had just delivered a knockout performance, he would take a friendly little jibe at those writers who had claimed that his talent had faded. But these moments of light good humor were rare now, for Frank was in combat mode with just about everyone.

In *Life with Jackie*, Irving Mansfield's book about his late wife, the actress-novelist Jacqueline Susann, Mansfield describes a nightmarish experience working with Sinatra as a producer of his television show, *The Frank Sinatra Show.*

Mansfield was a seasoned professional, and he believed in careful preparation and rehearsal. These were the days of *live* television, after all, when mistakes couldn't be cut and corrected. Sinatra, however, felt that one of his chief assets was being able to convey a sense of spontaneity to his audience and that repeated

rehearsals could become counterproductive. Inevitably, Mansfield and Sinatra clashed:

"I lived in hell for the next eight weeks," Mansfield wrote. "He [Sinatra] was impossible to work with—absolutely impossible. A real spoiled brat... Frank was always late, sometimes two and three hours late; he hated to rehearse and refused to discuss the weekly format."

During a rehearsal for the last Mansfield-produced Sinatra show, Mansfield asked Sinatra to go over a bit of business a second time because some of the technical aspects of a scene had not gone smoothly. "Listen, pal, I don't have time today to do it again, and I don't care what you like or don't like. You don't like me, either, do you?" Mansfield quoted Sinatra as saying. He said he replied, "Frank, as an artist, you are incomparable. Nobody can touch you. But where you're a failure is as a human being." Sinatra, Mansfield says, shouted at him that he was fired. Mansfield replied that he had already quit.

In the autumn of 1951 Universal-International decided to make a movie about an arrogant, surly crooner, who climbs to the top with the help of gangster friends. The film was called *Meet Danny Wilson* and it was a foregone conclusion who they wanted to play the lead. A star's salary at Universal was not what it was at MGM, but Sinatra needed the work. His all-suffering love interest in the movie was played by Shelley Winters.

In Winters' autobiography, *Shelley Also Known As Shirley*, the actress described the Sinatra of 1951 as follows: "Frank was in the process of divorcing Nancy to marry Ava Gardner.... Frank was truly impossible and so disturbed that he couldn't hear anything that anyone said to him, including the other actors, the crew, and the director, Joe Pevney. Everyone in Hollywood knew of his struggles 'to divorce or not to divorce' and the columnists as well as the industry were giving him a very bad time."

And Sinatra, according to Winters, was giving everyone around him a bad time in return. He became more surly than the character he was portraying. She recalls that at one point she became so enraged at his behavior that she slugged him and walked off the set.

DURING THE FILMING OF A SCENE OF *MEET DANNY WILSON* IN WHICH SINATRA KISSED COSTAR SHELLEY WINTERS, SINATRA GARNERED A BIT OF PRAISE. WHEN THE CAMERA STOPPED ROLLING, "SHELLEY SLAPPED FRANKIE ON THE BACK AND CONGRATULATED HIM," COLUMNIST SIDNEY SKOLSKY WROTE. "SHE TOLD HIM THAT IT WAS THE BEST SCREEN KISS SHE EVER HAD AND THAT SHE HAD DONE BUSINESS WITH RONALD COLMAN AND MONTGOMERY CLIFT. DURING THE ENTIRE SCENE THEY HAD A PLAYBACK GOING OF SINATRA'S NEW RENDITION OF "THAT OLD BLACK MAGIC," WHICH IS SUNG BY THE VOICE IN THIS MOVIE. SAID SINATRA, 'I GUESS I'M THE FIRST FELLOW WHO EVER KISSED A WOMAN AND SANG A SONG AT THE SAME TIME☆ '"

In Meet Danny Wilson (1951), Sinatra portrayed a singer controlled by the mob. He would later insist that the film was not autobiographical☆

YEARS LATER, IN 1965, AT AN AFFAIR HONORING ASSOCIATED PRESS COLUMNIST JIM BACON IN BEVERLY HILLS, SINATRA DELIVERED HIS OWN HILARIOUS VERSION OF HIS RELATIONSHIP WITH THE PRESS.

"I THINK IT'S ONLY FITTING I BE INVITED TO SPEAK TO A GATHERING OF NEWSPAPERMEN AND WOMEN, CONSIDERING THE MARVELOUS RELATIONSHIP I'VE ALWAYS HAD WITH THE PRESS," HE BEGAN BY SAYING. "MANY OF YOU MIGHT HAVE HEARD THAT I HAVE IN THE PAST BEEN HOSTILE AND BRUTAL TO MEMBERS OF THE FOURTH ESTATE. THESE ARE LIES, VICIOUS RUMORS STARTED BY A FEW DISGRUNTLED REPORTERS THAT I HAPPENED TO RUN DOWN WITH MY CAR.

"BUT I WANT TO SAY THAT WITH ALL OF MY COMPLAINING THERE HAVE BEEN MANY PERIODICALS THAT HAVE BEEN MORE THAN FAIR AND HONEST WITH ME, SUCH STERLING PUBLICATIONS AS *POPULAR MECHANICS*, *BOYS LIFE*, *THE SIMPLICITY PATTERN BOOK*☆ "

"Contrary to other Italians I have known since, he didn't hit me back. Maybe he went home and hit Ava Gardner."

In her book, however, Winters claimed that clashes with Sinatra occurred with regularity and that she finally determined that she would not continue working with him. On the second day of her walkout, she writes, she received a telephone call from Nancy Sinatra saying that if the picture was not completed, Frank would not be paid his $25,000 fee. "The bank might foreclose the mortgage on the house. My children are going to be out in the street. Please finish the picture."

The picture was completed and earned Sinatra the best critical reviews he had received to date. He was booked into the Paramount in New York, on a double bill with the movie, but the theater often had as many empty seats as filled ones. The movie was a dud.

Years later, Sinatra wrote of this period: "At thirty-eight years old, I was a has-been, sitting by a phone that wouldn't ring, wondering what happened to all the friends who grew invisible when the music stopped, finding out fast how tough it is to borrow money when you're all washed up. Yes, when 1953 slid down the pole in Times Square, my only collateral was a dream, a dream to end my nightmare."

Opposite: In the fall of 1950, Sinatra hosted Meet Frank Sinatra, a one-hour Sunday afternoon radio show on CBS. Here he interviews Metropolitan Opera star Mimi Benzell and seven-year-old New York schoolboy Johnny Scolle about their favorite recordings☆

SUCCESS IN HOLLYWOOD

Opposite: With Bing Crosby in front of the cameras for High Society *(1956).* **Left:** *With his diminutive golden friend, Oscar* ☆

From Oblivion to *Eternity*

In 1953, Columbia Pictures brought "the boldest book of our time"—From Here to Eternity—"honestly, fearlessly" to the screen. Perhaps the boldest element in producing the movie was putting Frank Sinatra in it.

Frank Sinatra knew he needed to land a role in a credible film in order to put the brakes on his downward spiral. Ava Gardner did her part, floating news items that she wanted to appear in a movie with her husband, that they were "looking for a great story." The "great story" of 1951 was the year's number one bestseller, James Jones' *From Here to Eternity*, a devastating depiction of the postwar army in Hawaii. Harry Cohn ("King Cohn") head of Columbia Pictures, had obtained the movie rights. Daniel Taradash was to convert Jones' novel into a screenplay, Fred Zinnemann was to direct, and Buddy Adler was to produce.

Sinatra was certain that the film would become every bit the sensation the book was. He also was certain that if he could land the role of Private Angelo Maggio, he'd be able to resuscitate his career. He arranged a meeting with Harry Cohn.

He had first met Cohn four years earlier, when he was still packing theaters as a performer. In those days, to paraphrase a Sinatra song, live entertainment and movies went together like a horse and carriage. A live show would be performed, there'd be an intermission, then a movie would be screened, there'd be another intermission, then the live show, and so on. So a movie on a bill with Sinatra could realize a big box office return even if it were a dud.

Miss Grant Takes Richmond, starring Lucille Ball and William Holden, was certainly no dud, but it wasn't exactly a blockbuster either. Cohn asked Sinatra if he could use his clout to have the comedy featured on the same bill with him at the Capitol Theater in New York. Sinatra saw the film, found it amusing, and told the management at the Capitol that he wanted the film booked into the theater during his engagement. The management balked, but Sinatra prevailed. The theater took in $122,000 during the first week of Sinatra's appearance. Cohn took an ad in *Variety* to announce that *Miss Grant Takes Richmond* had realized $122,000 at the box office in its first week in New York. Of course, he never mentioned that Sinatra was double billed with it.

Now, it was Sinatra's turn to ask a favor.

Columnist Earl Wilson, in his biography of Sinatra, says Cohn told him that the conversation during his meeting with Sinatra went like this:

SINATRA: Harry, I want to play Maggio.

COHN: You must be out of your fuckin' mind. This is an actor's part, not a crooner's.

SINATRA: Harry, you've known me for a long time. This part was written about a guy like me. I'm an actor. Give me the chance to act.... I've been gettin' $150,000 a week. Well, you can get your Maggio for my expenses.

COHN: ...Expenses?

SINATRA: A thousand a week, $750 a week, for nothin'. I've got to have it.

COHN: You want it that much, Frank?

SINATRA: I told you, it was written for me.

COHN: Well, we'll see, Frank, we'll see.

SINATRA: You're not turning me down then?

COHN: I was, but let's see, let's see. It's a wild idea.

Perhaps too wild for Cohn, who, according to Bob Thomas, author of *King Cohn*, suspected that if Sinatra appeared in *From Here to Eternity*, audiences might mistakenly think it was a musical.

COHN HAD BEEN HAVING OTHER CASTING PROBLEMS WITH *ETERNITY*. HE AND ZINNEMANN WANTED JOAN CRAWFORD AS THE FEMALE LEAD. CRAWFORD WAS INTERESTED—UNTIL SHE SAW THE UNGLAMOROUS OUTFITS SHE WOULD HAVE TO WEAR. SHE TOLD COHN THAT SHE WOULD NOT APPEAR IN ANY MOVIE DRESSED LIKE THAT.

AGENTS FOR OTHER STARS CALLED COHN. WHEN DEBORAH KERR'S AGENT PHONED HIM, THE IMAGE OF THE REGAL ENGLISH ACTRESS CAME TO HIS MIND AND WOULDN'T JIBE WITH THE IMAGE OF THE EARTHY KAREN HOLMES, THE *ETERNITY* CHARACTER.

"WHY, YOU STUPID SON OF A BITCH," COHN YELLED INTO THE TELEPHONE AT THE AGENT. "GET OUTTA HERE."

A FEW MINUTES LATER, ZINNEMANN AND TARADASH ARRIVED FOR A MEETING. COHN TOLD THEM ABOUT THE TELEPHONE CALL.

"YOU KNOW WHO THIS STUPID SON OF A BITCH SUGGESTED? DEBORAH KERR!"

ZINNEMANN AND TARADASH TURNED TO ONE ANOTHER, SMILED, AND SHOUTED, "WHAT A GREAT IDEA!"

THEY FOUND A STRONG ALLY IN COLUMBIA PRODUCER JERRY WALD, WHO HAD BEEN INSISTING ALL ALONG THAT CRAWFORD WOULD BE WRONG FOR THE PART. WHEN HE HEARD ABOUT KERR, HE URGED COHN ON ENTHUSIASTICALLY. "LET'S MISCAST SOMEBODY WHO IS *RIGHT* FOR THE PART!" WALD THEN SPENT THREE DAYS TALKING TO KERR ABOUT DITCHING HER LUCRATIVE CONTRACT WITH MGM. A FEW DAYS LATER, SHE WAS BRUSHING UP ON HER AMERICAN ACCENT.

COHN WAS INSISTENT THAT AT LEAST ONE OF COLUMBIA'S CONTRACT PLAYERS BE CAST IN THE ROLE OF THE PROSTITUTE (TURNED INTO A "HOSTESS" IN THE MOVIE). WHAT HE DID NOT EXPECT WAS THAT ZINNEMANN'S CHOICE WOULD BE DONNA REED, THE TOO-GOOD-TO-BE-REAL WIFE OF JIMMY STEWART IN *IT'S A WONDERFUL LIFE*.

With Donna Reed, rehearsing a scene for From Here to Eternity. *The Reed character was a prostitute in the original novel. Cleaned up for the movies, the role eventually led to Reed's starring for eight years in the consummately wholesome* The Donna Reed Show *on television. Both Sinatra and Reed won Oscars for* Eternity.

was not going to do the part because he had a commitment with Kazan and *Camino Real*. I sat silently by watching this extraordinary game of Ping-Pong between Cohn and Ava, which resulted in Harry promising that he would have a long talk with Buddy and yourself and try to persuade you gentlemen to use Sinatra."

Still, Sinatra heard nothing from Cohn or Adler or Zinnemann or anyone else connected with the production. In November, he flew to Africa, where Ava was shooting *Mogambo*, to be with her for their first wedding anniversary. And that's where he received word by cable that Columbia wanted him to appear in a screen test for the role of Maggio.

A day and a half later, Sinatra had returned to Hollywood. When he was handed the movie script and asked to read Maggio's drunk scene, he handed the script back, saying that he already knew it. On the first run-through—Sinatra was always at his best the first time around—he convinced all the doubters. In later years, everyone who witnessed the screen test recalled that they were all unanimous in their opinion—not only would Sinatra get the part; he'd get the Oscar.

He also got all of eight thousand dollars from Columbia, his entire salary for the role. But, as Sinatra had told Cohn, the part was worth more to him than the money.

Production of *From Here to Eternity* began in March and was completed less than eight weeks later. The political problems connected with completing the film started even before it ever went into production. Zinnemann and Adler first had to do battle with the censors at the Production Code Administration of the Motion Picture Association of America (MPAA), an office headed by Joseph Breen. They began receiving regular memos:

"Page 166: The expression, 'Get the hell out of the way' would be eliminated.

"Page 168: The same applies to the expression, 'you dirty sons —.' Likewise the expression, 'Nuts!' would be dropped."

On August 4, 1952, they received a letter from Breen in which he discussed the two leading characters in the story: "We feel it will be necessary to have a strong voice for morality by which their immoral relationship will be denounced and the proper moral evaluation of it expressed."

The same letter referred to the beach scene in which Burt Lancaster kisses Deborah Kerr as waves splash over them: "It would be well to have either Karen or Warden put on a beach robe or some other type clothing before they go into the embrace."

With Ava, during a stopover in London in November 1952, before flying on to Africa, where Ava was to begin filming Mogambo *and where they would both celebrate their first wedding anniversary*

What Cohn did not tell Sinatra was that he had already decided on the actor he wanted for the role: Eli Wallach. Wallach, however, wanted $20,000; Cohn had budgeted $16,000. The dickering went on, but Wallach soon tired of it and pursued other opportunities.

In the meantime, Sinatra mounted a massive campaign to nab the part that would have made Dolly Sinatra, the former Hoboken precinct worker, proud. He sent telegrams to Cohn, Adler, and Taradash, saying that "Sinatra is the best man for the part" and signing them "Maggio." Ava Gardner first lobbied Cohn's wife, then approached Cohn himself.

In a letter to Fred Zinnemann dated November 17, 1961, Jerry Wald told about being present when Gardner visited Cohn in 1952.

"[She] said she wanted Frank to play the role [of Maggio] and that if Harry would grant her this favor, she would try to break loose from one of her Metro commitments and make a picture for him. There were no guarantees on Ava's part, merely a promise. Harry was flattered and told Ava in front of me about the Eli Wallach test. He kept trying to pin her down to a definite commitment, but Ava was evasive. Harry knew perfectly well at that time that Eli Wallach

Indeed one of Harry Cohn's initial concerns about making the movie was that Jones' novel was simply too racy to be converted into a movie. He worried about the four-letter words, about the hookers, about the violence in the novel. But Taradash, who earned an Oscar for his work on the film, received high praise from critics for the screenplay, several of them saying they preferred it to the book. Jones himself had no objection to the removal of earthy language, which, he noted in a letter to Zinnemann, was accepted in novels but would seem so sensational on screen that it would detract from the story.

For the most part, things went well on the set in Hawaii. Zinnemann told an interviewer for *Collier's* magazine, "[Sinatra] played Maggio so spontaneously, we almost never had to reshoot a scene." Buddy Adler remarked, "He never made a fluff.... It was a case of the natural performer up against some great actors. The natural performer was better."

Sinatra soon formed a tight friendship with Montgomery Clift, the film's costar, who coached him endlessly. "I learned more about acting from him than I ever knew before," Sinatra said later. But Clift marveled at his pupil. While watching the "dailies" (scenes from the previous day's filming; also called "rushes") one day, he turned to Burt Lancaster and said tersely, "He's going to win the Academy Award."

Sinatra and Clift became drinking buddies, joined later by James Jones. The author was ostensibly on the set as a technical adviser, but his greatest contribution to the movie—aside from providing the story on which it was based—seems to have been coaching Clift how to box for a key scene; Jones had once been a Golden Gloves contender. An odd threesome: the down-on-his-luck crooner, fighting determinedly for survival; the tormented, homosexual actor whose good looks and intensity on- and offscreen could quicken the pulse of anyone who laid eyes on him; and the writer-boxer whose words on the page packed a wallop as solid as any his fists could deliver. The bonding glue for the three was booze. And accordingly, during the making of *From Here to Eternity*, Sinatra and his buddies drank themselves to eternity almost every night sitting in one another's hotel rooms, shut off from the rest of the world by their fame, shut off even from the tropical paradise outside their doors. It is not difficult to imagine the scene: Jones ranting on about the cosmic struggle, perhaps Clift correlating it to the conflict of great drama, Sinatra brooding about his relationship with Ava.

COLUMBIA NEEDED THE COOPERATION OF THE ARMY IN ORDER TO FILM PARTS OF *FROM HERE TO ETERNITY* AT SCHOFIELD BARRACKS IN HAWAII. DIRECTOR FRED ZINNEMANN AND PRODUCER BUDDY ADLER COURTED ARMY BRASS ASSIDUOUSLY AND EVENTUALLY WON THEIR ENTHUSIASTIC SUPPORT. IRONICALLY, WHEN THE FILM WAS FINALLY RELEASED, THE NAVY REFUSED TO SCREEN IT ABOARD SHIP, CHARGING THAT IT DISPARAGED A FELLOW SERVICE. THE ARMY, HOWEVER, SCREENED IT TO ROUSING RESPONSE ON BASES ALL OVER THE WORLD.

VIRTUALLY EVERY SHOCKING PUBLIC INCIDENT INVOLVING SINATRA TOOK PLACE WHEN HE WAS HIGH ON BOOZE, AS DID THE PRIVATE BRAWLS WITH FRIENDS AND LOVERS. BUT IF SINATRA EVER REGARDED HIS DRINKING AS A "PROBLEM," HE NEVER LET ON. INDEED, HE ALWAYS TOOK PRIDE IN CALLING HIMSELF A "SALOON SINGER." IN HIS NIGHTCLUB ACT, HE MADE NUMEROUS REFERENCES TO THE JOY OF DRINK. ON TELEVISION, HE WOULD HOLD A TEACUP ON HIS LAP, TAKE AN OCCASIONAL SIP FROM IT, AND AN EXPRESSION OF MISCHIEVOUS DELIGHT WOULD CROSS HIS FACE—SO THAT HIS AUDIENCE INSTANTLY CAUGHT ON THAT THAT WAS NO TEA IN THE TEACUP. WHEN HE RECEIVED A HUMANITARIAN OF THE YEAR AWARD FROM PRINCESS GRACE AT A VARIETY CLUBS INTERNATIONAL DINNER, HE REMARKED, "I PROPOSE A TOAST TO HER SERENE HIGHNESS PRINCESS GRACE AND TO HER ROYAL CROWN. AND TO MY CROWN ROYAL."

Burt Lancaster later told writer David Fury, "[Clift] and Frank Sinatra would get roaring drunk every night after filming. I spent so much time carrying them to their bedrooms and undressing them, putting them into bed night after night. To this day, Sinatra calls me 'mom.' He'll find me on my birthday, no matter where I am and say, 'Happy birthday, mom.'"

But Lancaster also wrote to Sinatra's daughter, Nancy: "Your father's fervor, his anger, his bitterness had something to do with the character of Maggio, but also with what he had gone through in the last number of years; a sense of defeat and the whole world

With Montgomery Clift on the set of From Here to Eternity. *Utter opposites in personality and outlook, they developed a tight bond during the making of the film that seemed vividly apparent on the screen.*

crashing in on him, his marriage to Ava going to pieces. All of these things caused this ferment in him, and they all came out in that performance. You knew that this was a raging little man who was, at the same time, a good human being."

From Here to Eternity premiered in August and quickly became the biggest moneymaker Columbia had ever seen. It opened opposite 20th Century Fox's *The Robe*, the first film to use the CinemaScope wide-screen process. It was a time when studios were looking to technical innovation to draw people away from their television sets and back into movie theaters. But *From Here to Eternity* showed that a tantalizing script and passionate performances could be an even bigger draw than big screens and stereophonic sound. (*From Here to Eternity* did employ a wide-screen process and stereo sound, but as *New York Times* film critic Bosley Crowther put it, "It does not need these enhancements. It has scope, power, and impact without them.")

Crowther had high praise for Sinatra. "Although it is a deviation from the norm," he wrote, "Frank Sinatra is excellent in the non-singing role of Angelo Maggio, a characterization rich in comic vitality and genuine pathos." Other critics, who only a few months earlier had dismissed Sinatra as finished, now waxed eloquent in describing his performance. *Time* magazine wrote: "Frank Sinatra does Private Maggio like nothing he has ever done before. His face wears the calm of a man who is completely sure of what he is doing as he plays it straight from Little Italy." Kay Proctor in the *Los Angeles Examiner* enthused: "For the first time on the screen he seems completely at ease and sure of himself and what he is doing....He is simply superb, comical, pitiful, childishly brave, pathetically defiant."

Oscar

On the night before the Academy Awards, Frank had a spaghetti dinner with Nancy and their children. They gave him a St. Genesius medal inscribed: "To Daddy. All our love from here to eternity."

Nancy Jr., thirteen, and Frank Jr., ten, accompanied him to the Oscars at the RKO-Pantages Theater in Hollywood on what was for him the most important night of his life.

WHAT IS STARTLING IS THAT DESPITE EVERYTHING, FRANK SINATRA AND HIS FIRST WIFE HAVE REMAINED FRIENDS. NANCY SR. ONCE WROTE, "IF I HADN'T HELD TO FRIENDSHIP WITH FRANK AND MADE HIM WELCOME IN OUR HOME, I COULDN'T HAVE LIVED WITH MY CONSCIENCE. CHILDREN NEED TWO PARENTS. WHENEVER THERE'S SOME SPECIAL PROBLEM OF DISCIPLINE, I'VE BEEN ABLE TO CALL THEIR FATHER AND SAY, 'I THINK THIS IS SOMETHING YOU SHOULD HANDLE. I CAN'T BE THE OGRE ALL THE TIME. AND ALWAYS, FRANK HAS COME OVER.'"

Arriving at the Oscars in 1946 with Nancy, literally stepping in the footsteps of the stars who preceded him. Sinatra performed one of the nominated songs that year. When, eight years late, he received his own Oscar for From Here to Eternity, *he was accompanied to the ceremony by Nancy Jr. and Frank Jr.*

The best supporting actor and actress of 1953: Frank Sinatra and Donna Reed, for From Here to Eternity.

pleted reading the list of nominees and tore open the envelope containing the name of the winner. Sinatra nervously rocked in his seat while his daughter tried to calm him.

"And the winner is...Frank Sinatra!"

The orchestra, on cue, flooded the theater with the theme of *From Here to Eternity.* Sinatra rose from his seat in the rear and glanced at Nancy Jr., who was now sobbing with happiness. For a minute, he hesitated, thinking that he ought to try to calm *her*, then Frank Jr. urged him down the aisle. On all sides of him, his peers in the industry were applauding and shouting, giving him the biggest standing ovation that he had heard since those early heady days at the Paramount. When he reached the stage, he hugged entertainer Donald O'Connor and kissed McCambridge. He received the golden statue and caressed it, and the audience continued to roar.

As the applause died down, Sinatra tried to speak. "Uh." The sound crept through the public-address system and out onto the television airwaves. "That's a clever opening," he said, abashed. The audience laughed. What was there to say? He looked around. "They're doing a lot of songs up here tonight, but nobody asked me." Laughter again. "I really, really don't know what to say, because this is a whole new thing. I've always done song-and-dance-man-type stuff. And I'm terribly pleased, and if I start thanking everybody, I'll do a one-reeler." More laughter and applause. A few more words, and finally: "I love you, though," and he left the stage. He would later say:

"God chose to smile on me.... Talk about being born again, it was one time in my life when I had such happiness I couldn't share it with another human being."

Protocol required Sinatra to proceed backstage at the Pantages, where he would be interviewed by the print media in one area, then be interviewed by newsreel and television broadcasters in another area, then be photographed in another area, then be shunted into several small dressing rooms where individual radio interviewers and columnists were ensconced. Sinatra, however, was not about to run that gauntlet. In fact, he later said, he even ducked out of the post-Oscar party. He decided just to take a walk: "Just me and Oscar! I think I relived my entire lifetime that night as I walked up and down the streets of Beverly Hills."

The newspapers the next day all ran different versions of the greatest-comeback-in-motion-picture-history story. Sinatra would later respond, "Just call it 'the Rise and Fall and Rise Again of Frank Sinatra.'"

The papers had said he was the favorite to win the best-supporting-actor Oscar. But winning an Oscar often has more to do with politics than performance. And Sinatra wasn't sure how his troubled public image might sway the vote. He wasn't even sure how his industry colleagues, who composed the Pantages audience that night, felt about him.

His doubts, however, must have faded when, as Mercedes McCambridge, the presenter of the Best Supporting Actor award, came to his name, a round of expectant applause broke out in the theater. Her distinctive voice sounded faintly ethereal as she com-

Sinatra, the Actor

The offers for movie and television roles, and the requests for personal appearances were now pouring in. It seemed to many observers that if Sinatra wanted a particularly juicy film role, he would be able to get it and set his own fee to boot. To an extent that was true, and Sinatra knew it. Unfortunately, the movie Sinatra wanted to make after *From Here to Eternity* was *On the Waterfront.* He felt the same about the role of Terry Malloy as he had about the role of Maggio—that it was a natural for him

(indeed, the exterior scenes of the movie were eventually shot in Hoboken, New Jersey) and that this time it would turn him into a contender for the Best Actor Oscar.

He arranged meetings with producer Sam Spiegel and Columbia Pictures' Harry Cohn. What happened at those meetings later became the crux of a lawsuit Sinatra filed against Cohn, Spiegel, and Columbia. Sinatra claimed in the suit that Cohn had verbally promised the Malloy role to him. Spiegel later claimed that he had always wanted Marlon Brando for the part but that he had offered Sinatra the role of the priest in *Waterfront* (Brando, after all, had been nominated three years in a row for Oscars; he finally won with *Waterfront*). Sinatra's $500,000 suit was later settled, but terms of the settlement were never revealed.

The billboards for Suddenly, Sinatra's first movie after From Here to Eternity, *were tawdry and off-putting, but the film, in which Sinatra played a shunned, alienated character bent on assassinating the president of the United States, seemed especially pertinent nine years later when a real-life character succeeded where Sinatra's onscreen character had failed.*

Not as a Stranger, which was followed by *Guys and Dolls*, which was followed by *The Man with the Golden Arm*, which was followed by *High Society*, and so on.

High Society united him for the first time on screen with his childhood idol, Bing Crosby. It also put him together with Grace Kelly. Kelly had recently accepted the marriage proposal of Prince Rainier of Monaco, and while the film was being shot, the prince bided his time at one of Howard Hughes' mansions in Beverly Hills, from which he rarely ventured forth. When reporters buttonholed him, he told them that he was opposed to his future wife continuing to work in films. She, meanwhile, joined him at the mansion every night after work on *High Society*. It was her first musical and her last film.

"Working with Bing Crosby and Frank Sinatra was simply marvelous," she told Nancy Jr. "They create a certain excitement and are two very strong personalities. So it was fascinating for me to be in the middle—watching the tennis match go back and forth from one to another with tremendous wit and humor— each one trying to outdo the other... Frank and I did two numbers... He has an endearing sweetness and charm as a person and an actor."

A bove: With Doris Day in Young at Heart *(1954), a musical version of* Four Daughters *(1938), the film that gave John Garfield his start. This was Sinatra's first musical after* Eternity *and is regarded by many critics as his best.* **Right:** *With Nancy Gates in* Suddenly☆

In the end, he followed up *From Here to Eternity* with *Suddenly*, in which he played a "nobody" wanting to make a name for himself by assassinating the president of the United States. Said *Newsweek:* "Sinatra superbly refutes the idea that the straight-role potentialities which earned an Academy Award for him in *From Here to Eternity* were one-shot stuff. In *Suddenly*, the happy-go-lucky soldier of *Eternity* becomes one of the most repellent killers in American screen history. Sneeringly arrogant in the beginning, brokenly whimpering at the finish, Sinatra will astonish viewers who flatly resent Bobbysoxer idols." *Cue* magazine commented that Sinatra's acting represented "a solid and richer talent than many suspected.... He holds the screen and commands it with ease, authority and skill."

Sinatra never regarded his move into straight acting as a wrenching turn. "Actors who can't sing can't switch to our side [singing]," he once said. "But there's no reason why a singer can't go dramatic. A singer is essentially an actor."

When he returned to making musicals with Warner Brothers' *Young at Heart*, costarring Doris Day, the same year, any doubt about his popular appeal vanished. The movie not only attracted big box office crowds at a time when television was crushing attendance, it also produced Sinatra's first smash hit record in six years.

He began alternating straight dramatic films with musicals. *Suddenly* was followed by *Young at Heart*, which was followed by

Brando and Sinatra

SINATRA WAS STILL STEAMING OVER BEING SUPPLANTED BY MARLON BRANDO IN *ON THE WATERFRONT* WHEN THE TWO WERE BROUGHT TOGETHER FOR THE MOVIE VERSION OF *GUYS AND DOLLS*.

MOREOVER, THEY EMPLOYED OPPOSITE ACTING METHODS. SINATRA ALWAYS STUDIED HIS SCRIPTS ASSIDUOUSLY IN ADVANCE IN ORDER TO DELIVER HIS BEST PERFORMANCE ON THE FIRST TAKE. "I DON'T BUY THIS TAKE AND RETAKE JAZZ," HE WAS ONCE QUOTED AS SAYING. "THE KEY TO GOOD ACTING ON THE SCREEN IS SPONTANEITY—AND THAT'S SOMETHING YOU LOSE A LITTLE WITH EACH TAKE."

BRANDO, HOWEVER, FOLLOWED THE METHOD, GRAPPLING WITH CHARACTERIZATION AND NUANCE OFTEN THROUGH DOZENS OF TAKES.

THE SINATRA-BRANDO HOSTILITIES BEGAN ON DAY ONE. WHEN THEY WERE INTRODUCED, BRANDO SAID AMICABLY, "FRANK, I'VE NEVER DONE ANYTHING LIKE THIS [A MUSICAL] BEFORE.... MAYBE I COULD COME TO YOUR DRESSING ROOM AND WE COULD JUST RUN THE DIALOGUE TOGETHER?" SINATRA REFUSED TO TAKE THE BAIT, REPLYING, "DON'T GIVE ME ANY OF THAT ACTORS STUDIO SHIT."

THEN, IN THEIR VERY FIRST SCENE TOGETHER, BRANDO WENT THROUGH 34 TAKES, GARBLING HIS LINES CARELESSLY. FINALLY, SINATRA LOST HIS COOL. "YOU SEE THAT CHEESECAKE?" HE YELLED, POINTING TO A PROP. "IF YOU DON'T GET IT RIGHT, I'M GOING TO MAKE YOU EAT THE WHOLE THING, EVERY FUCKING BIT OF IT! NOW DO IT RIGHT, GODDAMN IT!" BRANDO'S RESPONSE WAS TO INVOKE HIS FAMOUS SMIRK—AND BLOW THE TAKE YET AGAIN. SINATRA WALKED OFF, ACCOMPANIED BY HALF THE OTHER ACTORS ON THE SET.

GUYS AND DOLLS PROVED TO BE AN UTTER EMBARRASSMENT FOR BRANDO. DESPITE THE FACT THAT, AS THE ROMANTIC LEAD, SKY MASTERSON, HE WAS HANDED THE BEST BALLADS, HIS VOCAL DELIVERY WAS FLAT AND HIS DANCING WAS CLUMSY. SINATRA, MEANWHILE, PLAYED THE SECONDARY ROLE OF NATHAN DETROIT, A TWO-BIT GAMBLER. IF ANYTHING, THE CASTING SHOULD HAVE BEEN THE OTHER WAY AROUND.

MONTGOMERY CLIFT'S BIOGRAPHER, PATRICIA BOSWORTH, TELLS THE STORY OF HOW CLIFT WENT TO A NEW YORK PREVIEW OF *GUYS AND DOLLS* IN NOVEMBER 1955 BECAUSE, AS HE SAID, "I'M DYING TO HEAR MARLON AND SINATRA TRY AND SING TOGETHER." BOSWORTH SAYS THAT SHORTLY AFTER THE FILM BEGAN, CLIFT BEGAN CREATING A DISTURBANCE. "MARLON IS VOMITABLE," HE SAID ALOUD. "OH, LOOK AT POOR FRANK." FINALLY, AFTER THOSE AROUND HIM BEGAN SHUSHING HIM, HE ROSE AND ANNOUNCED, "THIS PICTURE SUCKS. LET'S GET OUT OF HERE." IN THE LOBBY, CLIFT CONTINUED HIS HARANGUE, AND THEN, UNEXPECTEDLY, SMASHED HIS FIST INTO A GLASS DISPLAY CASE IN WHICH PHOTOGRAPHS AND "ONE SHEETS" FROM THE MOVIE WERE POSTED.

With Marlon Brando, Jean Simmons, and Vivian Blaine (far right) in Guys and Dolls. *In discussing the making of the movie in his 1994 autobiography, Brando failed even to mention Sinatra.*

On the set of High Society *(1956) with Grace Kelly. The film, a musical remake of the 1940 hit* The Philadelphia Story, *was Kelly's last before becoming Princess Grace of Monaco*

Crosby and Sinatra also often wowed cast and crew with their ability to wrap up a scene quickly, often in one take, and brilliantly. Sammy Davis Jr. was on the set when they performed "Well, Did You Evah?" together. "It was natural," he wrote later. "They weren't going to hang around all day, and [director Charles] Walters was shrewd enough to realize it. They made one take. Everybody recognized that impromptu sparkle and spontaneity right away. It established the mood for the whole movie."

In 1956, *The Pride and the Passion* was a walloping debacle not only for Sinatra, but for everyone else involved, including costars Cary Grant and Sophia Loren and director Stanley Kramer.

WHILE WORKING ON THE SET OF *THE PRIDE AND THE PASSION*, SINATRA FREQUENTLY GREETED MALE CREW MEMBERS WITH, "HOW'S YOUR BIRD?" (THE "BIRD" IN QUESTION BEING THE MALE MEMBER). SOON AFTERWARD, THE CREW HEARD SOPHIA LOREN GREETING THEM THE SAME WAY. LOREN, WHO LATER SAID THAT MEETING SINATRA ON THE SET OF THE MOVIE WAS LIKE BEING IN A DREAM, ALSO MIMICKED SOME OF HIS OTHER EXPRESSIONS. SHE STARTLED THE CREW ONE DAY BY SAYING, "THAT WAS A FUCKIN' GAS!," ANOTHER ONE OF SINATRA'S FREQUENT UTTERANCES.

IN DONALD ZEC'S BIOGRAPHY OF SOPHIA LOREN, STANLEY KRAMER RECALLED THAT SINATRA ENJOYED TRYING TO BAIT LOREN, OFTEN REMARKING TO HER, "ALL RIGHT, HONEY, YOU'LL GET YOURS." FINALLY LOREN WENT TO KRAMER AND ASKED "WHAT MEANS THAT? WHAT MEANS, "YOU'LL GET YOURS?"

"I TOLD HER IT MEANS, 'HE'LL GET YOU, SOPHIA, HE'LL GET YOU.' WELL, EVEN THEN, WITH HER POOR ENGLISH, SOPHIA SHOWED SHE HAD A PRETTY GOOD SENSE OF HUMOR. ONE NIGHT, A VERY RAINY NIGHT, WE SERVED SUPPER IN THE TENTS. THE WINE WAS BEING POURED—I DIDN'T WANT IT BUT THE SPANIARDS WOULDN'T WORK WITHOUT IT—AND THERE WAS SOPHIA AT ONE END OF THE TABLE, SINATRA AT THE OTHER. FRANK WAS IN A BAITING MOOD. HE ROSE ONTO THE TABLE, LOOKED DOWN ON SOPHIA AND HE SAID, 'HEY, SOPHIA, YOU'LL GET YOURS,' BUT SHE WAS READY FOR HIM THIS TIME. SHE GOT UP ON A CHAIR AND SAID: 'NOT FROM YOU, YOU GUINEA SON OF A BITCH☆'"

The signs of doom were apparent almost from the outset. First, Kramer had casting problems: he wanted Marlon Brando but cast Grant instead; he wanted Ava Gardner but hired the virtually unknown twenty-one-year-old Italian actress Sophia Loren, who had never appeared in an American movie and who in fact couldn't speak English.

Kramer had never shot a cast-of-thousands movie before. He had never shot a movie overseas with extras and technicians whom he often had to address through interpreters. He was unfamiliar

With Sophia Loren in The Pride and the Passion, *a film that in fact provided neither.*

spend days waiting to be called to the set. He chided Kramer almost continuously about the delays, urging him to push ahead. The director seemed to understand and to sympathize with his impatient star. "He was away from his cronies, away from the mainstream," he told Zec. "He was in the middle of nowhere for weeks and weeks and weeks."

Finally, Sinatra told Kramer that he could no longer put up with the delays and was returning home. Kramer said that he responded, "You know, Frank, it's different if you are dealing with—in your own language—a fink or somebody who doesn't have the integrity or is basically just not a nice guy or a guy not worth his salt in his work. But in every case I have filled the bill right up to the end with you." Kramer recalled that Sinatra replied, "Don't you understand? Do you want me to throw myself out of the window?" He eventually remarked that Kramer had his lawyers and he had his and that they could work it all out. And he left Spain five weeks before the end of production.

Nearly six million dollars—an enormous budget back then—was riding on *The Pride and the Passion*. Sinatra's sudden departure threatened to sink the entire project. Kramer was beside himself with worry.

"Cary's stature as a human being came to the fore," he told Nancy Nelson in *Evenings with Cary Grant*. "He came to me and said, 'Look, life is filled with pitfalls and disappointments. You can let this ruin the entire situation or you can rally above it and be a mensch. That's what I'm counting on you to be.' He touched me very much. He said, "Whatever it takes, no extra charge to you. I will fill in.' That meant doing close-ups with coat hangers as the foreground because Frank Sinatra wasn't there. Sophia Loren cooperated, too. But it couldn't salvage the film because Sinatra was a key part of it. I finally settled with his agent for one week in Los Angeles. We used palm trees on a stage instead of finishing in Spain."

In a period of a little more than two years (1955–1957), Sinatra starred in eleven feature films: *Suddenly, Young at Heart, Not as a Stranger, The Tender Trap, Guys and Dolls, The Man with the Golden Arm* (which earned him an Oscar nomination), *Johnny Concho, High Society, The Pride and the Passion, The Joker Is Wild*, and *Pal Joey*. It is doubtful whether any other actor has ever appeared in as many movies in so short a period. Moreover, he costarred in a memorable musical production of Thornton Wilder's *Our Town* on television, which yielded the hit song "Love and Marriage."

In Johnny Concho, *a small, 84-minute, black-and-white western that was moving, but no trailblazer.*

with the Spanish countryside—"Windmillville," Sinatra called it—which could be hot and dry on one day, then become a rain-soaked quagmire the next.

It also became evident that although teaming Frank Sinatra with Cary Grant may have seemed like an act of genius to attract crowds to the theaters, the two were grossly miscast for their roles, something Kramer himself was to concede years later. Sinatra's Spanish accent sounded like something he had picked up from Desi Arnaz. As Sinatra spoke it, "yes" for example, turned into "jez." Before leaving for Spain, he had told columnist Hedda Hopper: "I engaged a guitarist named Gomez and gave him the script of *The Pride and the Passion*. I put him in a recording room and had him read my lines. I want to play this like a Spaniard trying to speak English instead of as an American trying to speak like a Spaniard trying to speak the language."

When Sinatra arrived on location in Spain, he seemed cheerful and helped keep the spirits of cast and crew up with his enthusiasm and verve.

But the playfulness and camaraderie slowly vanished as problem upon problem delayed production and as Sinatra was forced to

His other records during that time included "Young at Heart," "I've Got the World on a String," "A Foggy Day," "My Funny Valentine," "I Get a Kick Out of You," "Day In, Day Out," "Three Coins in the Fountain," "Just One of Those Things," "All of Me," "The Gal that Got Away," "Someone to Watch Over Me," "Don't Worry 'bout Me," and "Learnin' the Blues," all with Nelson Riddle. In 1954 *Metronome* magazine named him Singer of the Year, while *Downbeat* voted him Best Male Vocalist.

DURING SINATRA'S "GOLDEN" PERIOD HE TALKED ENTHUSIASTICALLY ABOUT PRODUCING HIS OWN FILM, *THE JAZZ TRAIN*. THE CAST WAS TO BE "ALL NEGRO," HE SAID, EXCEPT FOR HIM. ACCORDING TO SINATRA, IT WAS TO BE BASED ON A TRUE STORY ABOUT A GROUP OF AMERICAN JAZZ MUSICIANS WHO TRAVELED THROUGH EUROPE AFTER THE WAR. THE JAZZMEN'S "ANGELS" WERE GIs WHO SKIRTED AROUND A U.S. GOVERNMENT RULE THAT FORBADE SERVICEMEN FROM INVESTING MONEY OVERSEAS. "I'LL PLAY THE BOY WHO GOT THE IDEA AND ROUNDED UP THE FELLOWS TO BACK IT," SINATRA SAID. "NO TWO OF THE ANGELS KNEW WHO THE OTHERS WERE." HE TALKED ABOUT USING SAMMY DAVIS JR. AS THE CHOREOGRAPHER AND HAVING LOUIS ARMSTRONG COSTAR IN THE FILM ALONG WITH MEMBERS OF THE ACTUAL "JAZZ TRAIN."

SOMEHOW , THE ENTIRE PROJECT GOT DERAILED ALONG THE WAY☆

There is also the strange case of the television show that got produced to great acclaim, but somehow mysteriously disappeared.

To those who saw it, the musical version of Thornton Wilder's *Our Town* on *Producer's Showcase* in 1955 was not just Sinatra at his best, not even television at its best—it was show business at its best. Given its stellar participants, how could it have been otherwise? It was produced by Fred Coe, television's top producer of the time (he'd win an Emmy for *Producer's Showcase* in 1955). It was directed by Delbert Mann, who won an Oscar the same year for *Marty* and who directed many of the most memorable productions on television's landmark dramatic series, *Playhouse 90*. Besides starring Sinatra as The Stage Manager, it costarred Eva Marie Saint—fresh from receiving the Oscar for *On the Waterfront*—as The Girl. (She ended up receiving an Emmy nomination for her role

in *Our Town,* but lost to Mary Martin, who appeared in *Peter Pan* that year). And it introduced a young stage actor—Paul Newman in his first, and only, musical—as The Boy.

The music was written by Sammy Cahn and James Van Heusen, Sinatra's favorite writing team ("Three Coins in a Fountain," "The Tender Trap," "All the Way," "High Hopes," "Call Me Irresponsible," "My Kind of Town," "Come Fly with Me"). With *Our Town*, they won the only Emmy ever awarded for a song written for television, "Love and Marriage." Finally, the musical was scored by the inimitable Nelson Riddle, Sinatra's favorite arranger.

With Olivia de Havilland in Not as a Stranger *(1955). Although based on another bestseller, it failed to match the success of* Eternity☆

Sammy Cahn would later write: "The first time we sat down with Sinatra to play him the *Our Town* songs was in the home of his ex-wife Nancy, where he'd gone, Sinatra fashion, for a home-cooked meal. He kept following the songs intently. When Sinatra is in deep thought he has a habit of stroking his lower lip with the back of his thumb, and when we were finished, he looked up and said, 'Gee, it's good.' For him, that's high praise."

The actual production was broadcast live. Riddle and a fifty-piece orchestra were cloistered in a studio across the hallway, just as if they were simply providing a background score for a live drama— only in this case, their music was carried on small monitor speakers into the studio where the actors were performing. It all went off without a hitch.

The reviews the following day were positively rapturous. Abe Burrows called to say he wanted to produce *Our Town* on Broadway. Sammy Cahn would later write that the show was "blessed from the beginning."

But, as it turned out, the one lousy review was the one that counted the most—Thornton Wilder himself detested the production and refused to allow *Our Town* to be produced again. Moreover, he saw to it that every vestige of the original show— every tape, every script, every recording—was destroyed. *Our Town* was wiped off the historical map.

Sinatra wouldn't be heard on television singing "Love and Marriage" again until nearly forty years later, when the producers of the Fox network's *Married with Children* decided to use his 1955 recording of the song for its theme.

The End of Love

In 1953, Ava Gardner became pregnant. When she told her husband, he was elated. *Everything* was going right for him. If there was anything he loved more than being an entertainer, it was being a father.

But in an act that unquestionably doomed their relationship once and for all, Gardner, who would later write that she had felt she wasn't prepared to devote adequate time to being a mother, flew to London while Sinatra was away and had an abortion. (This was her second trip to London for an abortion; the first was in 1952,

while Frank was in Hollywood trying to persuade Harry Cohn to give him the part of Maggio in *From Here to Eternity*). In her autobiography, she would write: "Someone told him about what I was doing, because as long as I live I'll never forget waking up after the operation and seeing Frank sitting next to the bed with tears in his eyes. But I think I was right."

As for their marriage, however, it was now, as she put it, "past saving." Nevertheless, they remained married, and, by all accounts, Frank was still in love with Ava; their official divorce did not occur until 1957. Their problems had, without a doubt, led to the heavy drinking and resultant notoriety that had plagued him, enervated him, sent his career into a nosedive. But his urge to create and succeed survived this storm, and, it could be argued, was born of it.

The downside, of course, is that there was a Faustian penalty to be paid. Sinatra began displaying all the classic, upsetting characteristics of an alcoholic: aggression, contempt, impatience, jealousy, intolerance, irritability, moodiness, anger, vulgarity.

Sinatra continued to tell friends, "I know we could have worked it out." But at the same time he would say, "There is too much love for the basis for a real good marriage." He did what most psychiatrists agree is best for getting over a lost lover: he spent time with other people, especially his three children, and poured himself into his work. But he apparently could not bear to be without at least the image of Ava Gardner near him. He kept a picture of her pinned to his dressing room mirror on the sets of his movies. He commissioned the sculptor Jo Davidson to create a statue of her, which he displayed like a monument at his home. And her image (and absence) must undoubtedly have been etched in his mind as he recorded some of his most memorable torch songs of that period: "Call Me Irresponsible," "Softly, As I Leave You," "Just One of Those Things," "Don't Worry 'bout Me," "Tell Her," "The Gal that Got Away" ...and on and on.

Nearly forty years later, when his daughter Tina interviewed him while preparing a CBS miniseries about his life, he found talking about his relationship with Gardner awkward and upsetting. So did Tina.

"I didn't know how much the emotional scarring was. And it's deep. You know, that was really a tumultuous, tortured time for him. And when you observe someone's pain, if you love that person and you observe and you hear their pain, I don't care how old that pain is, if it's bad pain, it's like yesterday. But I learned a lot about the man as opposed to, you know, the father."

With Rita Hayworth in Pal Joey *(1957). The stage version had launched the career of Gene Kelly, but when the time came to adapt this story to the screen, Columbia went after Frank Sinatra.*

The Fall and Rise of Frank Sinatra

*O**pposite:** Enjoying a smoke with fellow Rat Packer Dean Martin.*

***Left:** The sign at the entrance to the Sands hotel in Las Vegas read, "A Place in the Sun." For a time, the Sands was just about Sinatra's only place in the sun. The recording industry, motion pictures, and television had all rejected him. But this rejection was not to last.*

The Kind You Can't Keep Down

The pose for which

Sinatra is perhaps

best remembered—

the rakishly tilted

head, the raincoat

over his shoulder,

the famous grin

The years just preceding the *From Here to Eternity* high were disastrous ones in Sinatra's recording career. Under Columbia Records' Mitch Miller, he was often reduced to cutting songs that were downright demeaning (although Miller insisted they were all "great"). No one bought them. When Sinatra's contract with Columbia expired, it was not renewed. And no other major label wanted him either.

But one person who remained a devoted fan was Miller's counterpart at fledgling Capitol Records: Alan Livingston. As Livingston

AT COLUMBIA RECORDS, SINATRA CLASHED WITH MITCH MILLER, THE DIRECTOR OF ARTISTS AND REPERTOIRE. MILLER WAS KNOWN FOR THE CHORAL HIT "THE YELLOW ROSE OF TEXAS" AND AS THE HOST OF *SING ALONG WITH MITCH*, WHICH AIRED ON NBC FROM 1962 TO 1966. MILLER'S FORTE WAS CATCHY COMMERCIAL NUMBERS, AND HE PERSUADED SINATRA TO RECORD A NUMBER OF THEM. IT WAS DURING THIS TIME THAT HE MADE WHAT IS NO DOUBT HIS MOST HUMILIATING RECORDING, A NOVELTY NUMBER CALLED "MAMA WILL BARK" WITH JENNIE LEWIS, WHO, AS DAGMAR, A DIMWITTED, BUXOM CAST MEMBER OF *BROADWAY OPEN HOUSE*, THE FIRST LATE-NIGHT NETWORK TELEVISION SHOW, HAD THE LOOKS AND DEPORTMENT OF AN OPERA SINGER—BUT NOT THE VOICE.

ON ANOTHER OCCASION, THE ARRANGER, COMPOSER, AND CONDUCTOR PAUL WESTON, WAS CALLED UPON BY MILLER TO PRODUCE AN ALBUM WITH SINATRA IN WHICH MILLER WANTED TO FEATURE "SOME HORRIBLE SONG," AS WESTON RECALLED IN A 1993 *TIME* MAGAZINE INTERVIEW, FEATURING "A [COUNTRY] GUITAR PLAYER WHO WAS FAMOUS FOR MAKING HIS GUITAR SOUND LIKE A CHICKEN." AT THE END OF THE SESSION, WESTON RECALLED, MILLER RUSHED PAST SINATRA "TO HUG THE CHICKEN PLUCKER." THREE MONTHS LATER, SINATRA AND MILLER PARTED COMPANY.

would later tell friends, no one besides Sinatra could make "old songs sound new, and new songs as if they were sung just for you."

At a staff meeting in February 1953, he introduced the company's new artist:

"Fellows, I want to tell you about a new artist we have just signed. He's not actually new, because a few years back he was a teenage idol. Then as all such stars must fade, he grew up and lost his audience. But he has tremendous talent. The kind of talent you can't keep down. So I signed him, and he is going to record for us."

Lloyd Dunn, a former Capitol executive, wrote in his book, *The Flip Side*, that when Livingston identified the "new artist" as Frank Sinatra, the reaction from the others at the meeting was a loud groan. He recalled that one person at the meeting remarked, "Sinatra? Mitch Miller dumped him at Columbia. He's had it!"

Another said, "He couldn't get a job singing on the Jersey Turnpike!" Still another shook his head and scowled, "God help us when we tell this to the dealers!"

Dunn at the time was in charge of album covers for Capitol, and he says that when Sinatra arrived for his first photo sessions, he was in the midst of making *From Here to Eternity* and had to fit the photo shoots around his studio schedule. Despite that, Dunn wrote, Sinatra was "eager to please." He recalled how Sinatra's most famous cover was shot:

"I faced him away from the camera and muttered to Ken Veeder, our photographer, 'Be ready to grab this—fast.' Then I gave Frank this routine:

"'You're walking down the street, going no place in particular. Suddenly a girl comes around the corner and passes you. She is obviously *gorgeous*. What a figure! What eyes! What... but she's walking away, out of your life! Look over your shoulder at her! Quick.'

"Frank looked. Ken snapped.

"When I saw the print, I stared at it for a long time. Never had I seen such an expression of sheer delight, lust, admiration, desire—you name it—all wrapped up into *one glance*.... What an actor!"

It was also Sinatra's ability to infuse the ballads he sang with a theatrical weight that gave his new conductor-arranger, Nelson Riddle, a direction for scoring them. Instead of laying them out, beginning, middle, and end, Riddle began creating a peak—like a dramatic climax—*before* the end. The tactic took advantage of Sinatra's natural acting ability and created some of his most evocative recordings, like "Nice 'N' Easy," "All the Way," and "My Funny Valentine."

The Rat Pack

By 1960—it was a very good year—Sinatra had the resources to call his own shots. That year, the Film Exhibitors of America voted him Top Box Office Star. When he began work at Columbia that same year on *The Devil at Four O'Clock*, he had final say over virtually every phase of production. His costar, Spencer Tracy, who had been stabled with him at MGM a decade earlier, remarked, "Nobody at Metro ever had the financial power Frank Sinatra has today." Tracy's explosive temperament was about as notorious as Sinatra's in those days, yet the film was completed without incident. Said Tracy: "He knew what he wanted and there were no fireworks, though some people said there would be."

Sinatra's wealth also allowed him to take his recording career in new directions. In fact, he was now able to set up his own record company, Reprise. He no longer had to record music formulated by some hotshot A&R man (A&R stands for "Artists & Repertoire"; A&R representatives are responsible for deciding which songs are recorded for a particular project). He could record anything he wanted to—and he did. Besides his signature torch songs and "swinging ballads," he was able to change tack to jazz, recording a vivid album of standards with Count Basie and an impressive collaboration with Duke Ellington. He even recorded a bossa nova album with Antonio Carlos Jobim after he sold Reprise to Warner in 1963.

As his own boss, Sinatra also had the power to prevent records that he was unsatisfied with from being released. Collectors who have kept track of Sinatra's recording sessions have noted such curious circumstances as the release of "I Left My Heart in San Francisco" by Reprise in September 1962, followed by its withdrawal from the market two weeks later.

And yet there was that "benevolent despot" aspect of his personality as well. From early in his career he surrounded himself with toadies who were willing to take a de facto the-king-can-do-no-

DURING THE LATE FIFTIES AND SIXTIES, SINATRA ALSO "COVERED" SEVERAL BALLADS OF SOME OF THE MORE FAMOUS ROCK SINGERS OF THE TIME—ALMOST AS IF TO SHOW THOSE SINGERS HOW SINGING THOSE SONGS *SHOULD* HAVE BEEN DONE. THERE IS NO QUESTION THAT SINATRA'S RECORDINGS OF PRESLEY'S "LOVE ME TENDER" OR GEORGE HARRISON'S "SOMETHING" ARE WONDERFUL INTERPRETATIONS OF THE ORIGINALS. HE WAS PROBABLY MOST SUCCESSFUL IN BLENDING THE SOUND OF CONTEMPORARY ROCK WITH HIS OWN BRAND OF POP WHEN HE RECORDED "STRANGERS IN THE NIGHT" IN 1966. BUT FOR THAT TUNE HE USED COMPOSER-ARRANGER ERNIE FREEMAN, WHO HAD SCORED HIT RECORDS FOR SUCH ROCK STARS OF THE PERIOD AS PAUL ANKA, BOBBY VEE, AND CAROLE KING.

With Spencer Tracy on the set of The Devil at Four O'Clock *(1961)*

But even Sinatra needed pals, and he was a member of a bona-fide gang. The members included the likes of Humphrey Bogart, Lauren Bacall, Sammy Davis Jr., "Prince" Michael Romanoff (a Beverly Hills restaurateur), David Niven, Judy Garland, Sid Luft, Swifty Lazar, Jimmy Van Heusen, Sammy Cahn, Shirley MacLaine, Peter Lawford, Joey Bishop, Dean Martin, and Kay Thompson (author of *Eloise*)—the Rat Pack, as they were called in the press, or, sometimes, the Clan.

If the Pack had a founding father, it was Humphrey Bogart, who lent his Holmby Hills home as a "clubhouse." The purposes of the group, according to Bogart, were "the relief of boredom and the perpetuation of independence," lofty goals for celebrities.

Just *belonging* to the group was a major accomplishment. Membership was by no means permanent; celebrities fell in and out of the group like gamblers at a Las Vegas blackjack table.

Peter Lawford had not even been on speaking terms with Sinatra when he was invited to join. Although they had worked together in films at MGM, they had had a falling out after Louella Parsons reported that Lawford had been spotted at a Beverly Hills restaurant having drinks with Ava Gardner. The headline had read, AVA'S FIRST DATE BACK IN THE U.S. IS PETER LAWFORD.

At two or three o'clock in the morning the day after that headline appeared, Lawford was awakened by a phone call. On the other end of the line was Frank Sinatra. According to Lawford, the conversation went like this:

SINATRA: What the fuck are you doing going out with Ava? You want both of your legs broken?
LAWFORD: But...but...but...but....
SINATRA: I don't want to hear that shit.
And he slammed down the phone.

Sinatra later agreed to speak to Milt Ebbins, who was also present when Lawford and Gardner met at the restaurant. Ebbins told him, "Frank, Peter didn't have a date with Ava. I was there. It was no date. We had a drink at The Luau, that's all. Her sister was there, too. There was nothing to it, Frank."

Sinatra asked Ebbins, "Are you sure?" And Ebbins replied, "I was there, Frank. Peter has no intention of seeing Ava. He'll never see her again."

Nevertheless, Sinatra, who knows how to hold a grudge, did not speak to Lawford again for eight years.

wrong pledge. The most well-known quote attributed to him in this vein is: "Don't tell me. Suggest. But don't tell me."

Certainly during his early years, he seemed to have had few friends, if any, who were willing to take him to task for displaying inconsiderate and abrasive behavior, fearing that he might turn on them, too. Within any group of peers, he was always treated as if he were the "chairman of the board."

Elvis & Frankie

In 1956 Elvis Presley introduced rhythm and blues into popular music, performing in a uniquely lusty style. He made no attempt to communicate the meaning of a lyric, and in fact hardly seemed to make himself under-stood—he slurred and grunted the lyrics with gusto. But it was not meaning he was after. What he brought to music was raw, unadulterated emotion.

Sinatra, like virtually all the established musicians of that time, reacted with contempt to Presley and the rest of the rock 'n' rollers, saying in 1957 that their music "fosters almost totally negative and destructive reactions in young people... My only deep sorrow is the unrelenting insistence of recording and motion picture companies upon purveying this most brutal, ugly, degenerate, vicious form of expression."

Yet there was no way of dodging Presley in those days, particularly if you were hosting television variety programs, as Sinatra continued to do. In 1960 Presley was discharged from the U.S. Army after a two-year stint. ABC producers approached Sinatra, suggesting that he devote a ten-minute segment of an upcoming special to welcoming Elvis home. Sinatra realized that he and Presley—who during two generations had touched off more hysteria than any living creatures since dinosaurs ruled the earth—could attract an enormous audience. Forget the hip gyrations and the mumbled singing. This could be big!

There was only one problem. Elvis' manager, Colonel Tom Parker, wanted $100,000 for his client. No one had ever received $100,000 to appear on a television special. Sinatra didn't hesitate, though; he agreed to pay Parker's price himself. The live special drew the highest ratings of any television show in five years. They did not perform together again, but ultimately the two of them—whose mercurial private personalities were alike in so many respects—took a liking to one another. Sinatra, in fact, became downright paternal toward the younger Presley. Years later he would remark:

"Elvis Presley was one of my dearest friends. And it always amazed me—I asked him once, 'Why didn't you get yourself a team of writers...and progress with what you were doing to something better than you were doing?' And he had no pure answer for me. He just said that he was comfortable in doing what he was doing and that he did that best. And, of course, I agreed with him. He did what he did best. But I wish that he had engaged songwriters to write him better material than what he was doing."

Elvis and Frank doing a number together in April 1960, just a couple weeks before Sinatra would welcome Elvis home from the army on national television.

It was hard to imagine an Elvis Presley record being bought because of the quality of the lyrics or musical composition. The *sound* was everything. And Sinatra, who worked to communicate the emotional content of every word and note, simply didn't get it, even though he has made half-hearted attempts to fit in, making some embarrassing stabs at recording rock music in the early 1960s—even putting out a "twist" album.

*W*ith Pat Lawford, sister of the president-to-be, in 1960.

The following year, Lawford and Sinatra wound up drunk in a hotel in Rome. Sinatra had been hoping to see Gardner there but she had been ducking him. Their marriage had already been over for two years, but Sinatra's torch had not yet been extinguished. Lawford later wrote:

"I don't know whether he sensed the compassion I felt for him, but suddenly he looked up from his drink bleary-eyed and said, 'Charlie'—which was the nickname he always used for me—'I'm sorry. I was dead wrong.' " Lawford said he responded, "Hey, I know it takes a lot for anybody, especially you, to say that. Let's not do that again. What a waste of time."

Lawford was soon accepted as a member of the Rat Pack. He performed in Las Vegas on the same bill with Sinatra, Sammy Davis Jr., Dean Martin, and Joey Bishop. They made several light-hearted, lightweight movies together. But, Lawford later wrote, "even as close as we got, I never had a feeling of permanence. I knew you could never rely on this impulsive, explosive, gregarious, generous, charming, petulant man for a real friendship."

But Lawford went on to say, "I don't want it to sound phony, but I consider it a privilege to live in the same era Frank's in. I do. I think he's a giant. Apart from that vast talent—we don't have to talk about that—he's got qualities of energy, imagination, kindness, thoughtfulness, awareness, all those qualities you try to find in yourself and hardly ever do."

Producer Arthur Julian, interviewed by James Spada for his book about Lawford, later remarked, "I used to feel kind of sorry for Peter. He felt that being accepted by Sinatra was so important."

The same could have been said about Sammy Davis Jr. Sinatra had been the first major entertainer to take Davis under his wing. He featured him in his stage shows, counseled him on his career, and protected him against blatantly racist industry practices. For all of that, and more, he earned Davis' unquestioning devotion—and awe. "He had the aura of king about him," Davis would later write about Sinatra.

Sammy Davis Jr. was an incredibly versatile all-around talent. He was a dancer of dazzling agility, often more spectacular in live performances than Kelly or Astaire were on screen. He could hold his own as a drummer in the best of bands. His ability to dramatize a song sold a lot of records, including such hits as "Hey There," "What Kind of Fool Am I," "I've Got to Be Me," and "Candy Man." His acting ability earned him lead roles in such Broadway shows as *Mr. Wonderful*, *Golden Boy*, and *Stop the World—I Want to Get Off*,

What brought them together again, it seems, was politics. In 1958 Lawford married Patricia Kennedy, the sister of Senator John Kennedy of Massachusetts. At a dinner for Senator Kennedy at the Lawfords' home, Frank Sinatra found himself seated directly across the table from the hosts. At one point, he looked at Mrs. Lawford, then at her husband, and remarked, "You know, I don't speak to your old man." It was enough to break the ice—finally.

not to mention the later Rat Pack films he made with Sinatra and Company. And he was a mimic who could reproduce the voices of famous performers as accurately as a tape recorder and caricature their physical idiosyncrasies with his body as deftly as noted illustrator Al Hirshfeld could with his pen. It was probably his uncanny ability to imitate Sinatra, both physically and vocally, that endeared him to "the chairman."

Sinatra and Davis had first met in 1940 when they were both struggling unknowns, sharing a bill at a Detroit theater. Five years later Sinatra was "the Voice," the star of *Your Hit Parade*, and Davis was still a struggling unknown.

In Los Angeles one night, Davis headed over to NBC and stood in a crowd of hundreds of Sinatra fans waiting for their idol to emerge from the studio following the *Hit Parade* broadcast. He

Backstage with Dean Martin and Sammy Davis Jr. at Carnegie Hall in 1963.

Frankie and Sammy

in a photo apparently

inscribed by Sinatra:

"Aw'right buddy—

Where's the Broad?"

"…Didn't you work with your old man and another guy? Yeah sure… why don't you come back next week and see the show? I'll leave a ticket for you."

The following week, Davis was leaving the NBC theater after the show when a studio guard approached him. "Mr. Sinatra wants you to come to his dressing room."

Backstage, Sinatra was surrounded by flatterers and friends. He eventually spotted Davis, said a few perfunctory words to him, and Davis left—to head back on the road with his father and his uncle, Will Mastin.

A few months later, they were appearing in Portland, Oregon, when Mastin received a telegram: OPEN CAPITAL THEATER NEW YORK NEXT MONTH, FRANK SINATRA SHOW, THREE WEEKS, TWELVE FIFTY PER.

As Davis later wrote in his autobiography *Why Me?*, "Frank took me completely under his wing." When their engagement in New York City ended, Davis recalled, Sinatra took him aside and made the following promise: "Anything I can ever do for you—you've got yourself a friend for life."

Some celebrities take political positions, contribute to causes, and wear badges in support of political candidates. Sammy Davis Jr. represented the embodiment of a cause for Sinatra and, on countless occasions, Sinatra saw to it that injustices done to his friend were righted.

It happened first in the early fifties, when Sinatra was struggling to keep his career alive. His teenage fans had deserted him, but he could still draw a crowd in nightclubs. He was booked at the Copacabana when one night some of his friends decided to catch his act and invited Davis, who had sometimes opened Sinatra's theater show, to join them. Drummer Buddy Rich, who had booked the reservations for the show, led the way. But at the door of the Copa they were stopped. The doorman gave Davis what he later described as "a meaningful look," then told the others, "Maybe if you go away and come back in a little while, they'll be able to find [your reservation]." They left the Copa without seeing the show.

The next day Davis spoke to Sinatra. Frank opened the conversation by saying, "You are coming to the club tonight, Charley [one of Sinatra's nicknames for Davis; he also called him Smokey]. I made the reservation, and you're walking in there alone."

"Look, Frank, I'd rather not. I appreciate…"

"We won't discuss it. Just be there. When something is wrong, it's not going to get right unless you fix it. I know it's lousy, Charley, but you've got to do it."

watched Sinatra appear through the backstage door and begin to move through the crowd of screamers, autographing their scraps of paper. After signing Davis', Sinatra looked up and said, "Don't I know you?"

"Well," said Davis, "we were on the same bill with you and Tommy Dorsey in Detroit." And no one who had seen Davis perform with his father and uncle ever forgot them, including Frank.

In *Why Me?*, Davis wrote that he thought as he walked into the Copacabana, "Even if it goes smoothly, if I get in and get a table... forcing my way in where I'm not wanted is even more degrading than being turned away. But I could never face Frank if I backed out. He was in a decline and he needed the Copa more than they needed him. Despite that, he was fighting for me."

Davis said that he entered the club, feeling "the stares, like jabs against my skin." When he joined Sinatra in his dressing room after the show, he wrote, Sinatra put an arm around him and said, "You did something good, Charley."

Shortly after Sinatra received his Oscar for *From Here to Eternity*, Davis was in a horrendous auto accident that cost him an eye. Sinatra was one of the first to visit Davis at the hospital in San Bernardino, California, where he lay brooding about the accident's possible effect on his career. "You're going to be all right," Sinatra assured him. Davis recuperated at Sinatra's home in Palm Springs.

---

*B*OGART AND HIS WIFE, LAUREN BACALL, WERE THE FOUNDERS OF THE RAT PACK, AND THEIR HOME IN THE HOLMBY HILLS, ADJACENT TO BEVERLY HILLS, WAS THE RATS' NEST. AS CHARISMATIC OFFSCREEN AS HE WAS ON, BOGART BECAME A KIND OF GURU FOR STRIVING HOLLYWOOD CELEBRITIES OF THE LATE FORTIES AND FIFTIES.

YOU ONLY NEED TO LOOK AT FRANK SINATRA'S FILMS TO SEE HOW HE WAS INFLUENCED BY BOGART. LONG AFTER BOGART WAS DEAD, SINATRA SEEMED STILL TO BE METAMORPHOSING INTO BOGIE'S IMAGE.

SINATRA'S VISITS TO HIS FRIEND BECAME EVEN MORE FREQUENT AFTER BOGART WAS DIAGNOSED WITH THROAT CANCER IN 1956. HE REGULARLY VISITED BOGIE IN THE HOSPITAL, OFTEN ACCOMPANIED BY OTHER MEMBERS OF THE PACK, ALL DOING THEIR BEST TO KEEP THE GOOD-TIME GOALS OF THE GROUP INTACT EVEN AS ONE OF THEM LAY DYING.

SINATRA WAS PERFORMING AT THE COPA IN JANUARY 1957 WHEN HE GOT THE NEWS OF BOGART'S DEATH. GRIEF-STRICKEN, HE CANCELED THE REMAINDER OF HIS PERFORMANCES, AVOWING LARYNGITIS. PRIVATELY, HE TOLD HIS AGENT, "I CAN'T GO ON. I'M AFRAID I WON'T BE COHERENT."

THERE WAS NOW A NEW LEADER OF THE PACK.☆

Three years later, when Sinatra's close friend, Humphrey Bogart—the founder of the Rat Pack— died, Sinatra was so devastated that he felt he could not go onstage at the Copa, where he was booked. He asked Davis to fill in for him.

In 1960 Davis asked Sinatra to be best man at his wedding to Mai Britt. Sinatra readily accepted. What neither of them considered, however, was that the marriage might become an issue in Senator John Kennedy's tight race against Richard Nixon for the presidency.

A news item of the time: "Public opinion experts say that when Frank Sinatra appears at pal Sammy Davis, Jr.'s interracial marriage, it will cost Kennedy as many votes, maybe more, as the crooner has been able to swing via his successful JFK rallies."

Davis later wrote that he knew that he had put Sinatra—and Kennedy—"on the spot." If Sinatra did appear as Davis' best man, it could cost Kennedy crucial votes, especially in the South. However, if he did not show up at the wedding, Kennedy would probably lose the votes of many liberals and blacks. Davis phoned Sinatra.

SINATRA: Hi ya, Charley, what's new?

DAVIS: Frank, we're going to have to put the wedding off a couple of weeks. You wouldn't believe the problems a poor soul has trying to get married.... I don't know when it'll be but I'll give you plenty of notice.

SINATRA: You're lying, Charley.

DAVIS: Look, it's best that we postpone till after the election.

SINATRA: You don't have to do that.

DAVIS: I want to. All the talk...

SINATRA: Screw the talk.

DAVIS: I know, but it's better this way.

SINATRA: I'll be there whenever it is. You know that, don't you?

DAVIS: I know that, Frank.

SINATRA: I'd never ask you to do a thing like this. Not your wedding. I'd never ask that.

DAVIS: That's why it's up to me to be saying it.

SINATRA: You're a better man than I am, Charley. I don't know if I could do this for you, or for anyone...

DAVIS: You've been doing it, haven't you?

There was a long silence on the line. And then Davis heard Peter Lawford's voice: "Frank can't talk anymore, Charley...it's beautiful of you."

Still, Mai Britt never approved of Davis' relationship with Sinatra. She once chastised her husband: "The way he treats you, the jokes, the way you kowtow to him."

Although Davis always managed to laugh off Sinatra's behavior, insisting even that *he* always invited it, there were times when it rankled. It also irritated him when he saw Sinatra treating others similarly. In fact, he had complained publicly about Sinatra's behavior during a Chicago radio interview in 1959.

"There are many things he does that there are no excuses for. Talent is not an excuse for bad manners.... It does not give you the right to step on people and treat them rotten. That is what he does occasionally."

Davis made those comments just after Sinatra had him written into a movie, *Never So Few*, set in Burma during World War II. Davis was to portray a member of a band of guerrillas and U.S. GIs fighting the Japanese, despite the fact that no blacks ever saw duty in Burma. When Sinatra heard about Davis' remarks, he wrote him out of the film.

Peter Lawford later wrote that Davis was "destroyed" by Sinatra's action and that he called frantically to say that Sinatra would not return his calls. Lawford later called Davis to tell him, "I talked to Frank, but he won't budge."

The falling-out did not last long. "Frank let him grovel for a while," Lawford wrote, "and then allowed him to apologize in public a few months later."

According to Nancy Sinatra, almost all of her father's famous fallings-out could have been avoided. Referring to the breach that occurred between him and Joey Bishop, she wrote: "Joey made a mistake many people, myself included, make in disputes with Frank Sinatra. Joey did not confront him directly. Joey did not explain the situation to him directly. He did not argue it out with him. Instead, Joey moved unprotesting out of Daddy's life.

"You've *got* to face Frank Sinatra. Tell him the truth. Battle it out. Yes, he'll get mad. And so will you. But you'll come to some conclusion. You can't be so in awe of him that you're awed right out of a relationship."

The problem, any number of his onetime friends might argue, is that Sinatra often closes or severs lines of communications. When he refuses to take your phone calls or respond to your mail, what do you do?

Those who have maintained long-term friendships with Sinatra would advise to wait a while, then try again.

 ennedy

With President Kennedy at the 1961 Inaugural Ball, which Sinatra produced.

Unlike most of the other performers of his era, Sinatra frequently put himself on the line — often at great risk to himself and usually generating a good deal of press — for what he believed in. When considering the ways that he did so, there can be little question that his mother's dedicated efforts on behalf of the Democratic party back in Hoboken were a powerful influence. But there also seems to have been the notion in Sinatra's mind that singing and acting were not enough to satisfy whoever guarded the gates of Heaven, that men were ultimately judged not by such things as how many records they sold or how many Oscars they earned but by whether their actions made a difference.

He became known for gifts to friends in need, countless performances at charity functions, and endowments to hospitals. His humanitarian awards eventually outnumbered his professional ones.

While in public life his imposing demeanor earned him the designation Chairman of the Board, his natural sympathies embraced the underdog. There were his early appeals for racial and ethnic tolerance; his support for Roosevelt, Truman, Stevenson, Kennedy, Johnson, and Humphrey; and his friendships with directors, writers, and other performers who were activists or liberal progressives. With Kennedy, however, Sinatra was naturally attracted to his politics and equally drawn in by a special aura around the senator who would be president.

In 1960 Sinatra's support of John Kennedy for president presented the Massachusetts senator with an awkward dilemma. Sure, Sinatra could raise thousands of dollars at fund-raisers for the Kennedy campaign. But Kennedy advisers viewed him as a loose cannon. They subtly impressed on Sinatra that if he was to be a part of their inner circle, as he clearly wanted to be, he would have to play by their rules.

It is hard to imagine Sinatra playing by anybody else's rules. But the prospect of being an intimate friend of the president of the United States represented for him ultimate acceptance and vindication. He would pay a heavy price in his effort to win that friendship.

In January 1960, the infamous blacklist barrier began to come down in Hollywood, as director Otto Preminger and actor Kirk Douglas publicly announced plans to hire the same blacklisted writer, Dalton Trumbo, for their upcoming films. They were harshly castigated by such organizations as the American Legion, the Catholic War Veterans, and the Hollywood-based Motion Picture Association for the Preservation of American Ideals. Shortly thereafter, Frank Sinatra stepped forward to make an announcement of his own. He had hired Albert Maltz, the writer of the much-lauded *The House I Live In*, to write the screenplay for his forthcoming production of *The Execution of Private Slovik*.

The same patriotic organizations that had denounced Preminger and Douglas now shifted their attention to Sinatra. These groups pointed out that Sinatra was a supporter of Senator John Kennedy for the Democratic presidential nomination and asked whether the senator approved of Sinatra's hiring "a known communist" to write his film.

For a while, Sinatra staunchly held his ground. He purchased a full-page ad in *Variety*, saying: "As the producer of the film I and I alone will be responsible for it. I accept that responsibility. I ask only that judgment be deferred until the picture is seen. ...I make movies. I do not ask the advice of Senator Kennedy on whom I should hire. Senator Kennedy does not ask me how I should vote in the Senate."

For all his liberal associations, Sinatra certainly found no fans among the Soviet leadership. In 1959 Soviet prime minister Nikita Khrushchev had visited the set where Sinatra was filming *Can Can*, watched one of the dance numbers and then, at a dinner in his honor that evening, proceeded to chastise Hollywood for promoting immorality. Clearly Khrushchev did not approve of the kind of movies Sinatra made.

Strangely, within just a few days, Sinatra knuckled under to the protesters. In another full-page advertisement in *Variety* he wrote, "Due to the reactions of my family, my friends, and the American public, I have instructed my attorneys to make a settlement with Albert Maltz and to inform him he will not write the screenplay for *The Execution of Private Slovik*. I had thought the major consideration was whether or not the resulting script would be in the best interests of the United States. Since my conversation with Mr. Maltz had indicated that he had an affirmative, pro-American approach to the story and since I felt fully capable as a producer of enforcing such standards, I have defended my hiring of Mr. Maltz. But the American public has indicated that it feels the morality of hiring Mr. Maltz is the more crucial matter, and I will accept the majority opinion."

In fact, there was no such "majority opinion," and it is difficult to explain what actually caused Sinatra to respond so uncharacteristically to the token protests that developed, mostly from the Hearst press, Hedda Hopper, and the American Legion. He in fact became the only filmmaker to back off as one producer after another began rehiring blacklisted writers. (Not Albert Maltz, however, who, after the Sinatra incident, was regarded as "too hot to handle" for another seven years.) Within weeks of Sinatra's capitulation, Otto Preminger announced that he had hired another member of the Hollywood Ten, Ring Lardner Jr., to write a screenplay.

It was thought that Sinatra was concerned about how his hiring of Maltz might be used to embarrass Senator Kennedy. It was almost certain that Kennedy would win the Democratic presidential nomination and face Vice President Nixon, who had made his reputation as the man who exposed Alger Hiss as a communist working in the upper echelons of the State Department.

But by 1960 even Harry Truman, who had imposed the Loyalty Oath for government workers, had condemned the Hollywood blacklist as something that "allowed the camel's nose under the tent and destroys the Bill of Rights." And shortly after he was elected president, John Kennedy himself provided the ultimate example when he strode through the Catholic War Veterans picket line in front of a Washington, D.C., theater to see *Spartacus.* Afterward he said that he had enjoyed the movie and thought it was a good film.

In January 1960 four members of the Rat Pack—Sinatra, Sammy Davis Jr., Peter Lawford, and Joey Bishop—got together in Las Vegas to perform together not only at The Sands, a hotel in which Sinatra owned a stake, but also in a movie, *Oceans Eleven.* In February, they were visited at The Sands by John Kennedy. In Dean Martin's suite one evening, Sinatra introduced Kennedy to Judith Campbell, who was later identified in a Justice Department report as a girlfriend of the Chicago gangster Sam Giancana. It is unclear whether Kennedy actually met any of the gangland characters who continued to frequent posh Las Vegas hotels like The Sands despite being officially barred. But as phone records showing numerous calls placed by Kennedy to Campbell from the White House later revealed, Kennedy and Giancana certainly had a mutual friend.

Sinatra remained the most prominent Hollywood celebrity in the Kennedy camp prior to the Democratic convention in Los Angeles that year. During the primary, he recorded a special version of his Oscar-winning song, "High Hopes" (from *A Hole in the Head*), that was played again and again during Kennedy's campaign in two key primaries in Wisconsin and West Virginia. Songwriter Sammy Cahn altered the lyric about the ant trying to move a rubber-tree plant to "K-E-double-N-E-D-Y,/Jack's the nation's favorite guy./Everyone wants to back/Jack/Jack is on the right track/and he's got high hopes."

During the campaign against Nixon, Kennedy accepted an invitation to stay at Sinatra's home in Palm Springs. Afterward, Sinatra placed an engraved plaque on the door of the guest room, reading: "John Fitzgerald Kennedy Slept Here."

A month after the election, Sinatra was asked to produce the inaugural gala in January. It was assumed that Sammy Davis Jr., who had also supported Kennedy's candidacy, would also participate in the gala. Certainly Davis assumed so. After receiving an invitation to the inauguration, he publicly announced that his performances at the Latin Casino in Camden, New Jersey, would be canceled on inauguration day. But on January 17, Davis received a phone call asking him not to come to Washington. The phone call came from JFK's personal secretary, Evelyn Lincoln, asking him to "understand" the president's position. He said he did.

In his book *Why Me?*, Davis discussed his reaction: "My hurt and embarrassment turned to anger at my friends, at Frank and Peter: why didn't they stand up for me? But I knew they had, to the extent they could."

Davis did not hear from Sinatra. He did receive a call from Peter Lawford.

"They talked the President into it," Lawford told him. "They said... 'We've got Southern senators, bigoted congressmen. They see you as too liberal to start with... If we have Sammy here, is he going to bring his wife? We can't ask him not to....' The President said,

'Okay, then dump it. Call Sam. He'll understand.'" Lawford also said that Robert Kennedy had supported him and had become so angry by the decision to "uninvite" Davis that he stormed out of the room.

A few months later, Kennedy dumped Sinatra (in a way) as well. Sinatra had hoped that Kennedy would continue to visit him in Palm Springs following his election. He renovated and expanded his home and added a helicopter landing pad (for Marine One). He even erected a pole for the presidential flag and installed a plaque on the door of the new "Presidential cottage" where he expected Kennedy to stay. But shortly after the election Sinatra received word that Kennedy would be staying at Bing Crosby's home when he next visited Palm Springs. Presidential adviser Ken O'Donnell later wrote that the problem was political: Kennedy could not be a guest in the same home where Sam Giancana had also stayed. It was another hope-you-understand kind of thing. In October, the president, apparently hoping to patch things up with Sinatra, politely hosted Sinatra at the Kennedy compound in Hyannis Port, Massachusetts.

The Price of Fame

In November 1963 Sinatra was in the midst of filming the third and last of the Rat Pack movies, *Robin and the Seven Hoods*, with Bing Crosby. The year before, Frank had done his "serious" movie—*The Manchurian Candidate*, in which he played a brainwashed assassin, earning virtually uncontested critical and popular acclaim. Now, he was filming a scene in a Las Vegas graveyard where the "hoods" were burying hood-incarnate Edward G. Robinson.

After lunch one day, the Rat Pack and Crosby gathered in Sinatra's trailer for drinks, when there was a knock on the door. "Turn on the radio," someone said. "There's something about the president being shot."

The words chilled the room colder than the icy November nights of Las Vegas. "It can be confirmed that President Kennedy has been shot in Dallas. His condition is not known at this time. He has been taken by ambulance to Parkland Memorial hospital ...."

Sinatra called a halt to the shooting that day and took a walk, by himself, in that cemetery, looking forlorn and uncharacteristically vulnerable.

Sammy Davis Jr. noted: "Two images I remember of Frank: Frank walking down Broadway in the fifties when nobody recognized him, when he was alone, no hat on, topcoat collar up. And the image of him walking—on that beautiful sunlit day—in a graveyard."

As if his world had not already been turned upside down by Kennedy's assassination, two weeks later, Sinatra's son, Frank Jr., was kidnapped.

It was positively eerie how much Frank Jr. sounded like his old man. "Better," the old man would insist, pointing out that his son had received a lifelong education in music, while he himself could not read a note.

The younger Sinatra had launched his musical career in September 1963 at the Americana Hotel in New York. Three months later, while performing at Harrah's Hotel in Lake Tahoe, he was abducted at gunpoint by three blundering numskulls who had long romanticized about kidnapping Frank Sinatra Jr. the way Mickey Rooney and Judy Garland once did about "putting on a show."

Sinatra Sr. had received threats from crackpots all his life. His children had also received menacing notes. But none of that really prepared him for the shock of learning that his son had actually become a kidnap victim. Sinatra had paid the price—and then some—for celebrity. But the price he would have to pay now took a toll far higher than the $240,000 ransom paid to the kidnappers.

Arriving at the New York benefit premiere for Von Ryan's Express *(1965) with daughters Tina (left) and Nancy Jr. (right)*

There had always been a tight bond between Sr. and Jr. As a child, the younger Sinatra always adored spending time with his father. At home, he would play his father's records over and over. Nancy Jr. recalled her father saying when Frankie was nine, "He's so like me it's frightening. If I stand in front of the fireplace with my hands behind my back, he does the same thing.... When I do a TV show, he quotes everything I said the next time I see him."

When Sinatra learned that his son had been kidnapped, he telephoned Attorney General Robert Kennedy. Kennedy called FBI director J. Edgar Hoover, who advised Sinatra on how to deal with the kidnappers. According to the deal Sinatra made with them, the money was to be delivered to an assigned spot. Frank Jr. was to be dropped off a few hours later. But the appointed time for Sinatra to pick up his son came and went, and there was no sign of the boy. Sinatra returned to Nancy Sr.'s home. "Do you know what Dad's face looked like?" Tina said to her older sister when he arrived. "I've never seen a face look like that."

Frank Sinatra Jr. was returned to his home a few hours later by a security guard who found him wandering around near the drop-off point—a birthday present for his father one day early. But the ordeal, according to Nancy Jr., took a terrible toll on her father's mental and physical health. He wrapped up filming of *Robin and the Seven Hoods* so fast that he did not include a Sammy Cahn–Jimmy Van Heusen song that Cahn thought was one of the best he had ever written for Sinatra (Cahn later called this omission "the one great disappointment with Frank Sinatra in my life"). He returned to Palm Springs to recover. A few days later he received a note from Jacqueline Kennedy. Nineteen sixty-three had been a terrible year, she wrote, according to Nancy Jr. The only good thing about it was that Frank Jr. was safe.

The Author Remembers

In October 1963, I produced a pilot for a television series called *Surf Scene U.S.A.*, starring Jan and Dean. It was a disastrous experience from the first day of shooting to the final contretemps: Just as the sales force arrived in New York to begin their marketing efforts, Dean Torrance (of Jan & Dean fame), admitted on the witness stand at the Frank Sinatra Jr. kidnapping trial that he not only was friendly with the kidnappers, who had told him about their plans before they committed the act, but for a time had stashed the ransom money in his shower as a favor to them. The Desilu salesmen decided that it wasn't a good time to try to push the show and returned home. A few months later, Jan Berry was involved in a serious accident that put him in the hospital for a few months. Later, he was in in an accident that ended his career. *Surf Scene U.S.A.* suffered a wipe-out.

Changing Directions

During the mid-sixties, the conflicts of the times came knocking on Frank Sinatra's door. The kind of music he loved and represented was becoming virtually passé. New songwriters didn't turn out lyrics like "I'm as restless as a willow in a windstorm" any longer. They wrote things like, "She loves you, yeah, yeah, yeah." Changes were taking place, and Sinatra, like everyone else in midlife, didn't know what they meant.

Throughout his career, he had had the opportunity to perform with all of the top singers of the day: Crosby, Cole, Como, Charles, Bennett, Shore, Armstrong, Presley. But in a special issue about the Beatles published by *Look* magazine in 1966, Sinatra was quoted as saying: "I could never sing with them. I wouldn't know how. They have completely different interpretations."

Not that Sinatra didn't try to understand the new music. In 1966, he recorded "Strangers in the Night," a Bert Kaempfert number with a loud guitar twanging over the strings; this tune became his first number one hit in nine years. He got little satisfaction, however, when "Strangers in the Night"—"doobie doobie doo"—ended up on the air topping the Beatles, the Rolling Stones, and the Troggs. Sinatra hated the song. The same year, however, Nancy Jr. recorded her first—and only—number one hit, "These Boots Are Made for Walkin'." Unquestionably, Sinatra got a bigger kick out of his daughter's success than he did out of his own.

At its best, his music, ever autobiographical, chronicled his venture into middle age. Songs like "September Song," "Last Night When We Were Young," "Hello Young Lovers," "It Was a Very Good Year," and "The September of My Years" seemed to be created to be performed at the funeral of his youth.

Meanwhile, he met Mia Farrow, who was five years younger than his older daughter and a veritable sixties flower child, and married her in 1966. But as complex a woman as Farrow appears to be today, she later said she was unable to cope with the complexities of Frank Sinatra. He was fifty; she was twenty. The marriage lasted barely two years.

Politically, Sinatra remained the loyal Democrat, supporting Lyndon Johnson. That also meant supporting Johnson's divisive policies in Vietnam. Sinatra seemed to link what he believed to be

the degradation of American music to a breakdown in American values. LSD, the antiwar movement, rock and roll—they were all part of the same tide. And this time, perhaps even his detractors agreed with him.

Many of his closest friends, however, were becoming part of that tide. By 1968 they were supporting the Democratic party's antiwar candidates. His daughter Tina became an activist for Eugene McCarthy, while he remained loyal to Hubert Humphrey. When Humphrey lost to Richard Nixon, Sinatra found himself strangely alienated.

Ironically, a Republican president seems to have had no misgivings at all about forming a close bond with Sinatra. Richard Nixon

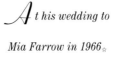

At his wedding to Mia Farrow in 1966.

With Mia on a rented yacht in Hyannisport, Massachusetts, in the late sixties ☆

invited him to the White House regularly. Vice President Spiro Agnew played golf with him in Palm Springs. In 1972 Sinatra supported the Nixon-Agnew ticket without reservation. Four years later, he helped raise money for Gerald Ford. And he has remained a Republican presidential supporter ever since.

The schism between Sinatra and his old political allies was never more strongly evident than at the Academy Awards ceremonies in 1975, when the Academy of Motion Picture Arts and Sciences, the organization that awards the Oscars, chose to honor *Hearts and Minds*, a memorable anti–Vietnam War film, for best

feature-length documentary. Sinatra was one of four hosts that year, and as he watched the two producers of the antiwar film make their acceptance speeches, his notorious anger welled up again.

Talks aimed at bringing the war to a negotiated end were taking place at that time in Paris between the Vietcong and the United States. In fact, the surrender of the Saigon government was only a few weeks away. *Hearts and Minds* producer Peter Davis took the microphone first to say, "It's ironic to get a prize for a war movie while the suffering in Vietnam continues." Then his partner, Bert Schneider, stepped forward to read a telegram from the Vietcong delegation at the Paris peace talks. "Please transmit to all our friends in America," the wire said, "our recognition of all they have done on behalf of peace and for the application of the Paris accords on Vietnam."

Sinatra at once descended on Howard Koch, the producer of the Oscars show—and, incidentally, the onetime executive producer of Frank Sinatra Enterprises—and demanded that the academy issue a public disclaimer. "This is too serious to let slide," he told Koch. He was joined by fellow emcee, Bob Hope, who began jotting down the academy disclaimer. A third host, Shirley MacLaine, an antiwar activist, prepared to battle Sinatra and Hope. "Don't you dare," she told Koch. And she began shouting at the two, asking what right they had to speak for the academy.

Koch was perplexed. Walter Mirisch, the president of the academy, was in the audience and could not be consulted. Now Koch was being confronted by the imposing figure of John Wayne, the actor who had once been the most prominent celebrity voice in support of the motion picture blacklist. Schneider, he said, was "a pain in the ass and outta line and [behaving] against the rules of the academy." Then actress Brenda Vaccaro pitched in to support MacLaine, observing that the academy didn't apologize the previous year when a streaker appeared on stage. Nor did it say anything when Marlon Brando sent an Indian representative to the awards ceremony in 1973 to officially reject his Best Actor Oscar for *The Godfather* (in protest of the treatment of Indians by Americans in general and the motion picture industry in particular).

Hope became impatient with the backstage debate. Flashing his notes in front of Koch, he said, "If you don't want to do it, I will."

"No," said Sinatra, "I'll do it." And he walked onstage and read the disclaimer: "We are not responsible for any political references made on the program. And we are sorry they had to take place this evening."

Offstage again, Sinatra was again accosted by Shirley MacLaine, an old friend and one of the few women ever to be invited into the ranks of the Rat Pack ten years earlier. "Why did you do that?" she asked. "You said you were speaking on behalf of the academy. Well, I am a member of the academy."

"Well, did you agree with that telegram?" Sinatra asked.

"It seemed like a very positive, friendly telegram to me," she replied.

The phone calls that flooded the network switchboard that night supported Sinatra better than three to one. Shirley MacLaine,

describing the backstage confrontation between herself and Sinatra and Hope, said the next day that "Bob Hope is so mad at me, he's going to bomb Encino."

The controversial incident drew attention away from a remarkable victory by Francis Ford Coppola, who received the best-picture and best-director Oscars that night for *Godfather II*, the first and only sequel in Oscar history ever to be so honored. Coppola later expressed his own outrage at the Sinatra-Hope disclaimer. "*Hearts and Minds,*" he said, "is not a musical comedy.... In voting for that picture the academy was sanctioning its message, which was in the spirit of Mr. Schneider's remarks."

From left to right: Dean Martin, Martha Hyer, assistant director William McGarry, Shirley MacLaine, and Sinatra on the set for Some Came Running.

Not the Retiring Kind

On March 21, 1971, at the age of fifty-five, Frank Sinatra did a preposterous thing. He announced his retirement. In a statement issued from his home in Palm Springs, he said that he needed an "opportunity for reflection, reading, self-examination...a long pause to seek a better understanding of changes occurring in the world."

"A long pause" turned out to be the operative words.

At the Academy Awards ceremony in April he received the Jean Hersholt Humanitarian Award. A few weeks later, the city of Los Angeles bestowed another humanitarian award on him.

His "retirement concert" was performed at a benefit for the Motion Picture and Television Relief Fund on June 13. Again the newspapers had been speculating about Sinatra's underlying motives, many of them concluding that health problems had overtaken him, forcing his retirement. But his performance that evening put the lie to that speculation. It was, by all accounts, nothing less than stunning, with Sinatra performing a chronology of top hits, closing with "My Way," "That's Life," and finally, "Angel Eyes," with its final line, "Excuse me while I...disappear."

His disappearance did not last long. In October 1972, he performed again at a fund-raising affair in Chicago for the Nixon-Agnew campaign. With Agnew present in the audience, Sinatra sang a special version of "The Lady Is a Tramp," retitled "The Gentleman Is a Champ." The following month another fund-raising affair featuring Sinatra raised $6.5 million for Bonds for Israel. At the dinner, Agnew, presenting Sinatra with a Medallion of Valor, called him "a legend in his own time, not only in the world of entertainment, but in the world of philanthropy."

Six months later, Sinatra was invited to perform at a White House state dinner for the Italian prime minister Giulio Andreotti. The invitation to the White House was long overdue. Except for Roosevelt, Democratic presidents whom he had embraced, worked for, and raised money for—without ever requesting a political favor—had regularly shunned him, concerned about how his notoriety might rub off on them.

Nixon later conceded that he had received letters from "some of the critics [he did not name them] objecting that because of his 'background' he should not have been invited. I thought this was nonsense...that he was one of the nation's outstanding performing artists and that our guest from Italy could not feel more complimented than to have him perform on that occasion."

"When I was a small boy in New Jersey," Sinatra said at the state dinner, "I thought it was a great boot if I could get a glimpse of the mayor. It's quite a boot to be here. I'm honored and privileged." No Democratic president had ever invited him to perform at the White House.

For a year after his retirement, the letters from disappointed fans poured in, begging him for "at least an album." Sinatra debated the idea and then, on April 29, 1973, he recorded three songs at the Goldwyn recording studios in Hollywood. Just what occurred at the session isn't clear, but a few days later Sinatra called the studio and asked that the master tapes be destroyed.

The suspicion is that Sinatra was simply unhappy with the way he sounded after being away from the microphones for a year. Nancy Jr. once quoted her father as saying—unrelated to the destroyed tapes incident—"When I haven't sung for a while, my reed gets rusty... You gotta pound on it for a while."

Nevertheless, he returned to the same studios a month later and began recording in earnest—three sides on June 4, three the following day, two on June 21, and four the day after that. In the end, those four days of work resulted in enough music for an

album. Several of the new songs were featured in a television special that November. The album and the special were called *Ol' Blue Eyes Is Back.*

His greatest comeback performance, however, came the following year at, appropriately enough, Madison Square Garden. In front of a live audience of twenty thousand and an international television audience believed to be the largest ever to watch an entertainment program until then, Sinatra's performance that night marked him as the mightiest champ that the historic Garden had ever seen. It was all the more remarkable for the fact that, although some three hundred fifty technicians were assembled for the show, as well as musicians, production staff, and talent (including Howard Cosell as the announcer) Sinatra never rehearsed a minute for it and in fact didn't arrive at the Garden until twenty minutes before the telecast.

The show was called "The Main Event" and it may have been the main event in Sinatra's career. "I have never felt so much love in one room in my life," he said later. After that, it was all a case of gilding the legend.

Take the following year, 1975, for example: A week of appearances with John Denver in Lake Tahoe in August drew 672,412 inquiries when it was advertised. A week of performances on Broadway in September with Count Basie and Ella Fitzgerald grossed approximately a million dollars. In London two months

Opposite, from left to right: Vice President Spiro Agnew, Italian Prime Minister Giulio Andreotti and his wife, Sinatra, Mrs. Ann Agnew, and President Richard Nixon and his wife, Pat, following a 1973 White House dinner for Andreotti. **Above:** *Around the time of his 1973 comeback, which resulted in both an album and a television special.*

Left to right:

Mrs. Barbara Sinatra,

Frank, Ronald Reagan,

and Nancy Reagan.

later, the London Palladium received 350,000 orders for 15,000 available tickets to a performance.

Or consider 1979: Upon its release, Sinatra's *Trilogy* album was dubbed "historic" by music critic Leonard Feather. It received six Grammy nominations. Former President Gerald Ford presented Sinatra with the International Man of the Year Award in Denver. An open-air appearance by Sinatra at the Pyramids in Egypt drew an audience of one thousand invited guests each night over three nights and raised $500,000 for charity. And he was the grand marshal in New York's Columbus Day Parade.

And so it continued. He produced Ronald Reagan's first Inauguration Gala in 1981, and Reagan, after taking office, had no fears about inviting Sinatra to the White House. In 1985, in fact, the president invited Frank there to bestow upon him the country's highest honor, the Presidential Medal of Freedom.

He received the Kennedy Center Honors for Lifetime Achievement; numerous honorary degrees from colleges; awards for philanthropy, including the Humanitarian Award from Variety Clubs International and the Life Achievement award from the National Association for the Advancement of Colored People. And his work received honors from such organizations as the Friars Club, the American Society of Composers, Authors and Publishers, the Simon Wiesenthal Center Fellows Society, the Songwriters Hall of Fame, Variety Clubs International, and the Boy Scouts of America.

In 1976 he was married for a fourth time — to Barbara Marx, former wife of Marx brother Zeppo — and he settled down, as they say. In an interview after the wedding, he remarked, "I really have found a new kind of tranquility. Barbara is a marvelous woman, and I have different kind of life now." He quit smoking, cut down on his drinking, and began exercising. It seems he became conscious of his own mortality.

The press did, too. If a lyric to a song was lost during a performance, a story would appear the next day suggesting that Sinatra was losing it all. If he used electronic prompting devices to keep the lyrics in front of him at all times, the press would imply that Sinatra's mind was failing him.

To be sure, Sinatra did not become all soft and bland. From time to time there were the flashes of the old, rambunctious fighter. Like the time in 1984 when a New Jersey gambling commissioner called him "an obnoxious bully" for lecturing a casino employee over the proper way to deal cards. Sinatra refused to perform in his native state again for more than a year. Or like the time that same year when he became incensed over an article in *The Washington Post* in which it was suggested that Ronald Reagan had become the "seventh member of the Rat Pack" and "the aura of gangland resonances" that surrounds Sinatra was discussed. Soon after, Sinatra was scheduled to appear on the television show *Entertainment Tonight*. As the cameras were focused on him, he interrupted the *ET* reporter's first question, glared at the gang of reporters taking notes off camera, and snarled, "Listen, I want to tell you something. You read the *Post* this afternoon? You're dead.... You're all dead." And like the time he threatened to sue Doonesbury cartoonist Garry Trudeau for a weeklong series of strips (published in June 1985) linking him with organized crime.

Controversy never deserted him. In 1986 he was the subject of Kitty Kelley's *His Way: The Unauthorized Biography of Frank Sinatra*. Kelley was paid $1.6 million for the 509-page book, which, she claimed, was exhaustively researched and involved interviews with 857 people. In interviews promoting the book, she displayed a large filing cabinet that she said was filled with her notes — more than a thousand folders. Yet many of the principals referred to in the book issued statements afterward calling Kelley's accounts lies and fabrications.

The image of Frank Sinatra that emerges from Kelley's book is one of a vicious tyrant, inevitably bullying and abusing everyone within range, and perpetrating unspeakable acts of brutality against women. That many of her allegations have been angrily refuted by several people she mentions in the book (some of whom she presumably interviewed) does not alter the fact that, until Sinatra himself decides to write his own memoirs, it will be the book of record about him.

In 1993 Sinatra's daughter Tina produced a "warts and all" television miniseries about her father, but, as with all such "docu-dramas," it is difficult to know when the "docu" leaves off and the "drama" begins.

In 1993 the man who had started out looking for a singing job at a roadhouse that had a "wire" connecting it to a radio station recorded an all-star album of duets, singing along with the likes of Barbra Streisand, Aretha Franklin, Natalie Cole, Bono, Julio Iglesias, Gloria Estephan, Tony Bennett, and others whose live voices were piped into the studio where he was recording over phone lines employing a new digital technology. This new record was called, appropriately enough, *Duets*. (It was followed in 1994 by a sequel, *Duets II*). The release and success of this record led the National Academy of Recording Arts and Sciences (NARAS), the organization that presents the Grammys, to honor Frank at thier 1994 Grammy Awards ceremony. Unfortunately, the ceremony was a debacle.

The Irish rock band U2 had just won a Grammy for *Zooropa*, which was named the best alternative album of the year. In the midst of his lurching acceptance speech, U2's frontman, Bono, promised "the young people of America" that "[w]e shall continue to abuse our position and fuck up the mainstream." The audience gasped. Garry Shandling, the event's master of ceremonies, said something about Bono being under the impression that he was "on cable," and CBS producers prepared to edit out Bono's obscenity for the tape-delayed telecast to the West Coast. But now, barely moments later, Bono was back on stage, this time clutching a sheaf of crumpled papers, to introduce Frank Sinatra and present him with NARAS's Lifetime Achievement Award.

Ah, the rites of commercial entertainment. The Grammy producers might have selected one of Sinatra's contemporaries to bestow the award on him—Dean Martin, say, or Tony Bennett, or even Ronald Reagan. But instead they chose Bono, who had not even been born when Sinatra was at his peak, who in fact was only a lad when the Beatles broke up, and whose only link to Sinatra was that he had recently been rounded up to sing a number with him on *Duets*. But Bono was up for the occasion. He passionately read his remarks, looking and sounding for all the world like an earringed beatnik who had landed like a time traveler from the fifties upon this glittery stage. His bohemian rhapsody to Sinatra borrowed its theme from Paul Anka's "My Way," but owed its soul to Sean O'Casey.

"Rock 'n' roll people love Frank," he said. "He has what we want: swagger and attitude. He's big on attitude, serious on attitude, bad attitude. Frank's the chairman of bad attitude. Rock 'n' roll players have been tough, but this guy is boss. The chairman of boss...heavier than the Empire State, more connected than the Twin Towers." And Bono continued in this vein, extolling Sinatra's temperament and self-image but never once praising the man's considerable talent and numerous musical accomplishments. If there could have been a single soul anywhere in the world watching the Grammys that night who had never heard of Frank Sinatra—an unlikely possibility—he might have concluded that Sinatra's "lifetime achievement" had been to develop a "bad" attitude. Finally, Bono's rambling came to an end. "I wouldn't mess with him. Would you?" The audience rose to its feet, shouting and applauding, and Sinatra walked on stage.

In tears, he shook Bono's hand, told the audience that theirs was "the best welcome I ever had," uttered a few of his trademark drinking jokes, extended his running gag about his friendship with Dean Martin, and then *they messed with him!* Susan Reynolds, Sinatra's publicist, told Michael Greene, president of NARAS, that

she was concerned that Sinatra might go on talking for an hour and asked CBS to cut him off. It did, with the telecast's director segueing ungracefully into a commercial.

The audience was stunned. So was emcee Garry Shandling. "That was a mistake," he said after the break, asserting that Sinatra should have been allowed to finish his speech. "This is live TV," Shandling then cracked, "and I'm sure Mr. Sinatra will get even by cutting this show off in another hour." Later, Shandling got off a better line. Lorena Bobbitt, he said, had just called to say "even she wouldn't cut off Sinatra."

For a man whose achievements in popular music overshadow those of any other performer, living or dead, the Grammy tribute was about as embarrassingly unfitting as Bono's earlier obscenity.

Hands across the generations: the Chairman of Boss and Bono at the 1994 Grammy Awards.

Even in his late seventies, Sinatra could still create hit records and pack arenas around the world.

Epilogue

And now the end is near,
And so I face the final curtain....

At this writing, Frank Sinatra is almost eighty years old. And the years sometimes conspire against him when he performs on stage. He has experienced fainting spells inside overheated venues. He sometimes begins to ramble confusedly on stage. But audiences forgive him. The lapses, after all, are infrequent, and when he's feeling fit, he still sounds superb. In fact, even when he's not, no one can explore the dimensions of a song as painstakingly as he can.

The long, breathless passages may be infrequent, and finding a suitable register for a song may take some calculating. And women may no longer scream during his songs. But they certainly sigh awfully loudly.

For those over fifty, his records provide the soundtrack for many of their memories. They were young during a time when popular music had style, class, and intelligence, and when orchestras were organic and could expand and contract around a singer's voice like a delicate, embroidered glove around a woman's hand.

Sinatra has fond memories of those days, too. "Those days and nights with the dance orchestras — I really miss them today. They were fun, they really were. We were young and strong, and everybody had a good time."

There have been few figures in the twentieth century who were more famous than Sinatra. There are a number of celebrities whom we recognize by only their first names — Bing, Elvis, Johnny, John-Paul-George-and-Ringo, Liza, Oprah, Madonna — but it is a quintessential mark of Frank Sinatra's fame that a Las Vegas hotel once took out an ad that read simply, "He's Back," along with a number to call for show reservations. No picture of Sinatra, no other identification. The reservations poured in.

The two words sum up much of Sinatra's life — from the moment that his grandmother plunged his head under a water faucet after birth, to his *From Here to Eternity* victory, to his return from retirement. One day, the two words might serve as the perfect epitaph: "He's back."

ibliography

Cahn, Sammy. *I Should Care: The Sammy Cahn Story.* New York: Arbor House, 1976.

Capra, Frank. *The Name Above the Title.* Indianapolis, Ind.: Macmillan, 1971.

Cogley, John. *Report on Blacklisting.* Pasadena, Calif.: The Fund for the Republic, 1956.

Csida, Joseph, and June Bundy Csida. *American Entertainment.* New York: Watson-Guptill Publications, 1978.

Davis, Sammy Jr. *Hollywood in a Suitcase.* New York: William Morrow and Company, Inc., 1980.

———, with Jane and Burt Boyar. *Why Me?* New York: Farrar, Straus & Giroux, 1989.

———, with Jane and Burt Boyar. *Yes, I Can.* New York: Farrar, Straus & Giroux, 1965.

Feather, Leonard. *The Encyclopedia of Jazz.* New York: Bonanza Books, 1960.

Gardner, Ava. *Ava, My Story.* New York: Bantam Books, 1990.

Glassman, Bruce. *Arthur Miller.* Englewood Cliffs, N.J.: Silver Burdett Press, 1990.

Harris, Warren G. *Cary Grant: A Touch of Elegance.* New York: Doubleday, 1987.

Hayman, Ronald. *Arthur Miller.* New York: Ungar, 1972.

Higham, Charles. *Ava.* New York: Delacorte Press, 1974.

Hirschhorn, Clive. *Gene Kelly.* New York: St. Martin's Press, 1974.

Howlett, John. *Frank Sinatra.* New York: Simon & Schuster, 1979.

Jewell, Derek. *Frank Sinatra.* Boston: Little, Brown, 1985.

Kelley, Kitty. *His Way: The Unauthorized Biography of Frank Sinatra.* New York: Bantam Books, 1986.

LaGuardia, Robert. *Monty: A Biography of Montgomery Clift.* New York: Arbor House, 1977.

Lawford, Patricia Seaton. *The Peter Lawford Story.* New York: Carroll & Graf Publishers, Inc., 1988.

Manchester, William. *The Glory and the Dream.* New York: Bantam Books, 1974.

Mansfield, Irving, with Jean Libman Block. *Life with Jackie.* New York: Bantam Books, 1983.

Manso, Peter. *Brando.* New York: Hyperion, 1994.

Peters, Richard. *The Frank Sinatra Scrapbook.* New York: St. Martin's Press, 1982.

Rockwell, John. *Sinatra, An American Classic.* New York: Rolling Stone Press, 1984.

Salinger, Pierre. *With Kennedy.* New York: Doubleday & Company, 1966.

Shaw, Arnold. *Sinatra: The Entertainer.* New York: Putnam, 1982.

Simon, George T. *The Best of the Music Makers.* New York: Doubleday & Company, 1979.

Sinatra, Nancy. *Frank Sinatra, My Father.* New York: Doubleday & Company, 1985.

Sorenson, Theodore C. *Kennedy.* New York: Bantam Books, 1966.

Spada, James. *Peter Lawford: The Man Who Kept the Secrets.* New York: Bantam Books, 1991.

Taylor, Robert. *Fred Allen: His Life and Wit.* Boston: Little, Brown, 1989.

Thomas, Bob. *King Cohn.* New York: Putnam, 1967.

Un-American Activities in California. The (California) Senate Fact-Finding Committee on Un-American Activities, Third, Fourth, and Fifth Reports. Sacramento, Calif.: 1947.

Walker, Leo. *The Wonderful Era of the Great Dance Bands.* New York: Doubleday & Company, 1964.

Wilson, Earl. *Sinatra: An Unauthorized Biography.* New York: New American Library, 1976.

Winters, Shelley. *Shelley Also Known As Shirley.* New York: William Morrow & Co. Inc., 1980.

Zec, Donald. *Sophia.* New York: David McKay Company, Inc., 1975.

essionography

1939–1942

New York City; February 3, 1959
Our Love (demo disc)

With Harry James
(all released on Columbia unless otherwise noted; all arranged by Andy Gibson)
New York City; July 13, 1939
From the Bottom of My Heart; Brunswick, Columbia (alternate take)
Melancholy Mood
New York City; August 17, 1939
My Buddy
It's Funny to Everyone But Me
New York City; August 31, 1939
Here Comes the Night
All or Nothing at All
Chicago; October 13, 1939
On a Little Street in Singapore
Who Told You I Care
Hollywood; November 8, 1939
Ciribiribin
Every Day of My Life

With Tommy Dorsey
(all released on Victor unless otherwise noted)
Chicago; February 1, 1940
The Sky Fell Down (arr. Axel Stordahl)
Too Romantic

New York City; February 26, 1940
Shake Down the Stars
Moments in the Moonlight
I'll Be Seeing You
New York City; March 4, 1940
Say It
Polka Dots and Moonbeams (arr. Axel Stordahl)
New York City; March 12, 1940
The Fable of the Rose (arr. Axel Stordahl)
This Is the Beginning of the End
New York City; March 29, 1940
Hear My Song Violetta
Fools Rush In
Devil May Care
New York City; April 10, 1940
April Played the Fiddle
I Haven't Time to Be a Millionaire
Imagination
Yours Is My Heart Alone
New York City; April 23, 1940
You're Lonely and I'm Lonely (The Dorsey Sentimentalists)
East of the Sun, with band chorus (arr. Sy Oliver); Bluebird
Head on My Pillow; Bluebird
It's a Lovely Day Tomorrow
New York City; May 23, 1940
I'll Never Smile Again, with the Pied Pipers (arr. Fred Stulce)
All This and Heaven Too
Where Do You Keep Your Heart?
New York City; June 13, 1940
Whispering, with the Pied Pipers; Bluebird, Victor
New York City; June 27, 1940
Trade Winds
The One I Love, with the Pied Pipers (arr. Sy Oliver)
New York City; July 17, 1940
The Call of the Canyon
Love Lies
I Could Make You Care
The World Is in My Arms
New York City; August 29, 1940
Our Love Affair
Looking for Yesterday
Tell Me at Midnight
We Three (arr. Sy Oliver)
New York City; September 9, 1940
When You Awake
Anything
New York City; September 17, 1940
Shadows on the Sand
You're Breaking My Heart All Over Again
I'd Know You Anywhere
Hollywood; October 16, 1940
Do You Know Why?
Hollywood; November 11, 1940
Not So Long Ago
Stardust, with the Pied Pipers (arr. Paul Weston)
New York City; January 6, 1941
Oh Look at Me Now, with the Pied Pipers & Connie Haines (arr. Sy Oliver)
New York City; January 15, 1941
You Lucky People You (arr. Sy Oliver)
New York City; January 20, 1941
I Tried

Dolores, with the Pied Pipers (arr. Sy Oliver)
Without a Song (arr. Sy Oliver)
New York City; February 7, 1941
Do I Worry, with the Pied Pipers
Everything Happens to Me
New York City; February 17, 1941
Let's Get Away From It All, with the Pied Pipers, Connie Haines & Jo Stafford (arr. Sy Oliver)
New York City; May 28, 1941
I'll Never Let a Day Pass By
Love Me as I Am
This Love of Mine (arr. Axel Stordahl)
New York City; June 27, 1941
I Guess I'll Have to Dream the Rest, with the Pied Pipers (arr. Axel Stordahl)
You and I (arr. Sy Oliver)
Neiani, with the Pied Pipers (arr. Axel Stordahl)
Free for All, with the Pied Pipers
New York City; July 15, 1941
Blue Skies, with band chorus (arr. Sy Oliver)
New York City; August 19, 1941
Two in Love
Pale Moon
New York City; September 18, 1941
I Think of You
How Do You Do Without Me?
A Sinner Kissed an Angel
New York City; September 26, 1941
Violets for Your Furs (arr. Heinie Beau)
The Sunshine of Your Smile
Hollywood; December 22, 1941
How About You?
Hollywood; January 19, 1942
(four sides without Dorsey; arr. and conducted by Axel Stordahl; released on Bluebird)
The Night We Called It a Day
The Lamplighter's Serenade
The Song Is You
Night and Day
Hollywood; February 19, 1942
Snooty Little Cutie, with the Pied Pipers & Connie Haines (arr. Sy Oliver)
Poor You (arr. Axel Stordahl)
I'll Take Tallulah, the Pied Pipers & Jo Stafford (arr. Sy Oliver)
The Last Call for Love, with the Pied Pipers (arr. Axel Stordahl)
Hollywood; March 9, 1942
Somewhere a Voice Is Calling (arr. Sy Oliver)
New York City; May 18, 1942
Just as Though You Were Here, with the Pied Pipers (arr. Axel Stordahl)
New York City; June 9, 1942
(arr. Axel Stordahl)
Take Me
Be Careful My Heart, with the Pied Pipers
New York City; June 17, 1942
In the Blue of Evening (arr. Axel Stordahl)
Dig Down Deep, with the Pied Pipers
New York City; July 1, 1942
(arr. Axel Stordahl)

There Are Such Things, with the Pied Pipers
Daybreak
It Started All Over Again, with the Pied Pipers
New York City; July 2, 1942
Light a Candle in the Chapel (arr. Axel Stordahl)

The Columbia Years: 1943–1952
New York City; June 7, 1943
(with the Bobby Tucker Singers, arr. Axel Stordahl)
Close to You
You'll Never Know
New York City; June 22, 1943
(with the Bobby Tucker Singers)
Sunday, Monday Or Always (arr. Alec Wilder)
If You Please
New York City; August 5, 1943
(with the Bobby Tucker Singers, arr. Alec Wilder)
People Will Say We're In Love
Oh What a Beautiful Mornin'
New York City; November 3, 1943
(with the Bobby Tucker Singers)
I Couldn't Sleep a Wink Last Night
The Music Stopped
New York City; November 10, 1943
(with the Bobby Tucker Singers)
A Lovely Way to Spend an Evening
The Music Stopped
New York City; November 13, 1944
(arr. Axel Stordahl)
There's No You
White Christmas, with the Bobby Tucker Singers
New York City; November 14, 1944
(arr. Axel Stordahl)
If You Are But a Dream
Saturday Night
New York City; December 1, 1944
(arr. Axel Stordahl)
I Dream Of You
I Begged Her, with the Ken Lane Singers
What Makes The Sunset
I Fall In Love Too Easily, with piano solo by Dave Mann
New York City; December 3, 1944
(arr. Axel Stordahl)
The Cradle Song
Ol' Man River
Stormy Weather, with the Ken Lane Singers
The Charm of You
Hollywood; December 19, 1944
(arr. Axel Stordahl)
Embraceable You
When Your Lover Has Gone
Kiss Me Again
She's Funny That Way
Hollywood; January 29, 1945
(arr. Axel Stordahl)
My Melancholy Baby
Where Or When, with the Ken Lane Singers
All The Things You Are, with the Ken Lane Singers
Mighty Lak' A Rose

Hollywood; March 6, 1945
(arr. Axel Stordahl)
I Should Care
Homesick That's All, with the Ken
   Lane Singers
Dream, with the Ken Lane Singers
A Friend of Yours, with the Ken Lane
   Singers
Hollywood; May 1, 1945
(arr. Axel Stordahl)
Put Your Dreams Away
Over the Rainbow, with the Ken Lane
   Singers
You'll Never Walk Alone, with the Ken
   Lane Singers
If I Loved You
Hollywood; May 16, 1945
(with the Charioteers, arr. Axel
   Stordahl)
Lily Belle
Don't Forget Tonight Tomorrow
I've Got a Home in that Rock
Jesus Is a Rock (in a Weary Land)
New York City; May 24, 1945
(arr. Xavier Cugat)
Stars In Your Eyes
My Shawl
Hollywood; July 30, 1945
(arr. Axel Stordahl)
Someone to Watch Over Me
You Go to My Head
These Foolish Things
I Don't Know Why
Hollywood; August 22, 1945
(arr. Axel Stordahl)
The House I Live In
Day By Day
Nancy
You Are Too Beautiful
Hollywood; August 27, 1945
(with the Ken Lane Singers, arr. Axel
   Stordahl)
America the Beautiful
Silent Night
The Moon Was Yellow
I Only Have Eyes for You
New York City; November 15, 1945
Just an Old Stone House (arr. Mitch
   Miller)
New York City; November 19, 1945
(arr. Axel Stordahl)
Full Moon and Empty Arms
Oh What It Seemed to Be
New York City; November 30, 1945
I Have But One Heart (arr. Axel
   Stordahl)
New York City; December 7, 1945
(arr. Axel Stordahl)
A Ghost of a Chance
Why Shouldn't I?
Try a Little Tenderness
Paradise
Hollywood; February 3, 1946
(arr. Axel Stordahl)
All Through the Day
One Love
Two Hearts Are Better than One
How Cute Can You Be?
Hollywood; February 24, 1946
(arr. Axel Stordahl)
From This Day Forward
Where Is My Bess?
Begin the Beguine
Something Old, Something New

Hollywood; March 10, 1946
(arr. Axel Stordahl)
They Say It's Wonderful
That Old Black Magic
The Girl that I Marry
I Fall in Love with You Every Day
How Deep is the Ocean?
Home on the Range
New York City; April 7, 1946
*Soliloquy, Parts 1 & 2 (*arr. Axel
   Stordahl)
Hollywood; May 28, 1946
(arr. Axel Stordahl)
Soliloquy, Parts 1 & 2
Somewhere in the Night
Could 'ja, with the Pied Pipers
Five Minutes More
Hollywood; July 24, 1946
(arr. Axel Stordahl)
The Things We Did Last Summer
You'll Know When It Happens
This Is the Night
The Coffee Song
Hollywood; July 30, 1946
(arr. Axel Stordahl)
Among My Souvenirs
I Love You
September Song
Blue Skies
Guess I'll Hang My Tears Out to Dry
Hollywood; August 8, 1946
(arr. Axel Stordahl)
Adeste Fideles
Lost in the Stars
Jingle Bells, with the Ken Lane
   Singers
Falling In Love with Love
Hollywood; August 22, 1946
(arr. Axel Stordahl)
Hush-A-Bye Island
*There's No Business Like Show
   Business*, with chorus
(Once Upon a) Moonlight Night
Hollywood; October 15, 1946
(arr. Axel Stordahl)
Poinciana
Why Shouldn't It Happen to Us
Hollywood; October 24, 1946
(arr. Axel Stordahl)
Time After Time
It's the Same Old Dream, with Four
   Hits & A Miss
I'm Sorry I Made You Cry
Hollywood; October 31, 1946
(arr. Axel Stordahl)
The Brooklyn Bridge
I Believe
I Got a Gal I Love
Hollywood; November 7, 1946
The Dum Dot Song, with the Pied
   Pipers (arr. Axel Stordahl)
*All of Me (*arr. George Siravo)
It's All Up to You, with Dinah Shore
   (arr. Axel Stordahl)
My Romance, with Dinah Shore (arr.
   Axel Stordahl)
New York City; December 15, 1946
*Always (*arr. Axel Stordahl)
*I Want to Thank Your Folks (*arr. Axel
   Stordahl)
That's How Much I Love You, with the
   Page Cavanaugh Trio (arr. Page
   Cavanaugh)

You Can Take My Word for It Baby,
   with the Page Cavanaugh Trio (arr.
   Page Cavanaugh)
Sweet Lorraine, with the Metronome
   All Stars (arr. Sy Oliver)
Hollywood; January 9, 1947
(arr. Axel Stordahl)
Always
I Concentrate on You
My Love for You
Hollywood; March 11, 1947
(arr. Axel Stordahl)
Mam'selle
Ain'tcha Ever Comin' Back?, with the
   Pied Pipers
Stella by Starlight
Hollywood; March 31, 1947
(arr. Axel Stordahl)
There But for You Go I
Almost Like Being in Love
Hollywood; April 25, 1947
(with Dinah Shore, arr. Axel
   Stordahl)
Tea for Two
My Romance, with chorus
Hollywood; June 26, 1947
(arr. Axel Stordahl)
*Have Yourself a Merry Little
   Christmas*
Christmas Dreaming
Hollywood; July 3, 1947
(arr. Axel Stordahl)
*Have Yourself a Merry Little
   Christmas*
Christmas Dreaming
The Stars Will Remember
Hollywood; July 23, 1947
*It All Came True (*arr. Axel Stordahl)
Hollywood; August 11, 1947
(arr. Axel Stordahl)
That Old Feeling
If I Had You
The Nearness of You
One for My Baby
Hollywood; August 17, 1947
(arr. Axel Stordahl)
But Beautiful
A Fellow Needs a Girl
So Far
Hollywood; September 23, 1947
It All Came True, with Alvy West and
   the Little Band (arr. Alvy West)
New York City; October 19, 1947
*Can't You Just See Yourself
   (*arr. Dick Jones)
*You're My Girl (*arr. Axel Stordahl)
*All of Me (*arr. George Siravo)
New York City; October 22, 1947
(arr. Axel Stordahl)
I'll Make Up for Everything
Strange Music
Laura
New York City; October 24, 1947
(arr. Tony Mottola)
My Cousin Louella
We Just Couldn't Say Goodbye
S'posin'
New York City; October 26, 1947
(arr. Axel Stordahl)
None But the Lonely Heart
The Song Is You
Just for Now
New York City; October 29, 1947
(arr. Axel Stordahl)

What'll I Do
Poinciana
Senorita
The Music Stopped
New York City; October 31, 1947
(arr. Axel Stordahl)
Mean to Me
Spring Is Here
Fools Rush In
New York City; November 5, 1947
(arr. Axel Stordahl)
When You Awake
It Never Entered My Mind
I've Got a Crush on You, with
   trumpet solo by Bobby Hackett
New York City; November 9, 1947
(arr. Axel Stordahl)
Body and Soul, with trumpet solo by
   Bobby Hackett
I'm Glad There Is You
New York City; November 25, 1947
*I Went Down to Virginia (*arr. Axel
   Stordahl)
If I Only Had a Match
New York City; December 4, 1947
(arr. Axel Stordahl)
If I Steal a Kiss
Autumn in New York
Everybody Loves Somebody
New York City; December 8, 1947
(arr. Axel Stordahl)
*A Little Learnin' Is a Dangerous
   Thing, Parts 1 & 2*, with Pearl
   Bailey
Ever Homeward
Hollywood; December 26, 1947
(arr. Axel Stordahl)
But None Like You
Catana
Why Was I Born?
Hollywood; December 28, 1947
(arr. Axel Stordahl)
O Little Town of Bethlehem, with the
   Ken Lane Singers
It Came Upon the Midnight Clear,
   with the Ken Lane Singers
White Christmas
For Every Man There's a Woman
Help Yourself to My Heart
Santa Claus Is Comin' to Town
Why Was I Born? (alternate take)
Hollywood; December 30, 1947
(arr. Axel Stordahl)
If I Forget You
Where Is the One?
When Is Sometime?
Hollywood; March 16, 1948
(prerecorded in Hollywood, December
   9, 1947; arr. Axel Stordahl)
*It Only Happens When I Dance
   with You*
A Fella with an Umbrella
Hollywood; April 10, 1948
Nature Boy, with the Jeff Alexander
   Choir (arr. Jeff Alexander)
New York City; December 15, 1948
*Once in Love with Amy (*arr. Mitchell
   Ayres)
Hollywood; December 15, 1948 (night)
(with the Phil Moore Four, arr. Phil
   Moore)
Why Can't You Behave
Bop Goes My Heart

Hollywood; December 16, 1948
*Sunflower (*arr. Axel Stordahl)
Hollywood; December 19, 1948
(arr. Axel Stordahl)
Comme Çi Comme Ça
No Orchids for My Lady
While the Angelus Was Ringing
Hollywood; January 4, 1949
(with the Phil Moore Four, arr. Phil
   Moore)
If You Stub Your Toe on the Moon
Kisses and Tears
Hollywood; February 28, 1949
(arr. Axel Stordahl)
Some Enchanted Evening
Bali H'ai, with chorus
Hollywood; March 3, 1949
(arr. Axel Stordahl)
The Right Girl for Me
Night After Night
Hollywood; April 10, 1949
(arr. Axel Stordahl)
The Hucklebuck, with the Ken Lane
   Quintet
It Happens Every Spring
Hollywood; May 6, 1949
(arr. Axel Stordahl)
Let's Take an Old Fashioned Walk,
   with Doris Day & the Ken Lane
   Singers
Just One Way to Say I Love You
New York City; July 10, 1949
(arr. Hugo Winterhalter)
It All Depends on You
Bye Bye Baby, with the Pastels
Don't Cry Joe, with the Pastels
New York City; July 15, 1949
If I Ever Love Again, with the Double
   Daters (arr. Hugo Winterhalter)
Hollywood; July 21, 1949
(arr. Morris Stoloff)
Just a Kiss Apart
Every Man Should Marry
The Wedding of Lili Marlene
Hollywood; September 15, 1949
(arr. Jeff Alexander)
That Lucky Old Sun, with chorus
Mad About You
Stromboli
Hollywood; October 30, 1949
(with the Modernaires, arr. Axel
   Stordahl)
The Old Master Painter
Why Remind Me?
Hollywood; November 8, 1949
(arr. Axel Stordahl)
Sorry, with the Modernaires
Sunshine Cake, with Paula Kelly
Sure Thing, with the Modernaires
Hollywood; January 12, 1950
(with the Jeff Alexander Choir,
   arr. Axel Stordahl)
God's Country
Sheila
Chattanoogie Shoe Shine Boy
Hollywood; February 23, 1950
(with the Modernaires, arr. Axel
   Stordahl)
Kisses and Tears, with Jane Russell
When the Sun Goes Down
New York City; March 10, 1950
*American Beauty Rose (*arr. Mitch
   Miller)

New York City; April 8, 1950
Peach Tree Street, with Rosemary Clooney (arr. George Siravo)
New York City; April 14, 1950
(arr. George Siravo)
Should I?
You Do Something to Me
Lover
New York City; April 24, 1950
(arr. George Siravo)
When You're Smiling
It's Only a Paper Moon
My Blue Heaven
The Continental
New York City; June 28, 1950
(with the Mitch Miller Singers, arr. Mitch Miller)
Goodnight Irene
Dear Little Boy of Mine
New York City; August 2, 1950
Life Is so Peculiar, with Helen Carroll & the Swantones (arr. Percy Faith)
New York City; September 18, 1950
(arr. Axel Stordahl)
Accidents Will Happen
One Finger Melody
New York City; September 21, 1950
(arr. Axel Stordahl)
Remember Me in Your Dreams, with the Whipoorwills
If Only She'd Look My Way
London by Night
New York City; October 9, 1950
Come Back to Sorrento (arr. Axel Stordahl)
April in Paris (arr. Axel Stordahl)
I Guess I'll Have to Dream the Rest, with the Whipoorwills (arr. Axel Stordahl)
Nevertheless, with trumpet solo by Billy Butterfield (arr. George Siravo)
New York City; November 5, 1950
Let It Snow, Let It Snow, Let It Snow, with vocal quartet (*arr. Axel Stordahl*)
New York City; November 16, 1950
(arr. Axel Stordahl)
Take My Love
I Am Loved
You Don't Remind Me
New York City; December 11, 1950
(with Rosemary Clooney, arr. Axel Stordahl)
Love Means Love
Cherry Pies Ought to Be You
New York City; January 16, 1951
(arr. Axel Stordahl)
Faithful, with vocal chorus
You're the One, with piano solo by Stan Freeman
New York City; March 2, 1951
(arr. Axel Stordahl)
Hello Young Lovers
We Kiss in a Shadow
New York City; March 27, 1951
(arr. Axel Stordahl)
I Whistle a Happy Tune
I'm a Fool to Want You
Love Me
New York City; May 10, 1951
(arr. Axel Stordahl)
Mama Will Bark, with Dagmar, imitations by Donald Bain

It's a Long Way from Your House to My House
Hollywood; July 9, 1951
(with the Harry James Orchestra, arr. Ray Coniff)
Castle Rock
Farewell, Farewell to Love
Deep Night
Hollywood; January 7, 1952
(arr. Axel Stordahl)
I Could Write a Book, with the Jeff Alexander Choir
I Hear a Rhapsody, with the Jeff Alexander Choir
Walkin' in the Sunshine
Hollywood; February 6, 1952
(arr. Axel Stordahl)
My Girl
Feet of Clay
Don't Ever Be Afraid to Go Home
Hollywood; June 3, 1952
Luna Rossa, with the Norman Luboff Choir (arr. Axel Stordahl)
The Birth of the Blues (arr. Heinie Beau)
Azure-Te (Paris Blues) (arr. Axel Stordahl)
Tennessee Newsboy (arr. Axel Stordahl)
Bim Bam Baby (arr. Axel Stordahl)
New York City; September 17, 1952
Why Try to Change Me Now (arr. Percy Faith)

The Capitol Years: 1953–1962

Los Angeles; April 2, 1953
Lean Baby (arr. Heinie Beau)
I'm Walking Behind You (arr. Axel Stordahl)
Don't Make a Beggar of Me (arr. Axel Stordahl)
Los Angeles; April 30, 1953
(arr. Nelson Riddle)
I've Got the World on a String
Don't Worry 'Bout Me
I Love You
South of the Border
Los Angeles; May 2, 1953
(arr. Nelson Riddle)
Anytime, Anywhere
My One and Only Love
From Here to Eternity
I Can Read Between the Lines
Los Angeles; November 5, 1953
(arr. Nelson Riddle)
A Foggy Day
My Funny Valentine
They Can't Take That Away from Me
Violets for Your Furs
Los Angeles; November 6, 1953
(arr. Nelson Riddle)
Like Someone in Love
I Get a Kick Out of You
Little Girl Blue
The Girl Next Door
Los Angeles; December 8, 1953
(arr. Nelson Riddle)
Take a Chance
Ya Better Stop
Why Should I Cry Over You?
Los Angeles; December 9, 1953
(arr. Nelson Riddle)

Rain (Falling from the Skies)
Young at Heart
I Could Have Told You
Los Angeles; March 1, 1954
(arr. Nelson Riddle)
Day In, Day Out
Last Night When We Were Young
Three Coins in the Fountain
Los Angeles; April 7, 1954
(arr. Nelson Riddle)
Sunday
Just One of Those Things
I'm Gonna Sit Right Down and Write Myself a Letter
Wrap Your Troubles in Dreams
Los Angeles; April 19, 1954
(arr. Nelson Riddle)
All of Me
Jeepers Creepers
Get Happy
Take a Chance on Love
Los Angeles; May 13, 1954
(arr. Nelson Riddle)
The Gal That Got Away
Half as Lovely (Twice as True)
It Worries Me
Los Angeles; August 23, 1954
(with vocal chorus, arr. Nelson Riddle)
When I Stop Loving You
White Christmas
The Christmas Waltz
Los Angeles; September 23, 1954
(arr. Nelson Riddle)
Don't Change Your Mind About Me, with chorus
Someone to Watch Over Me
You My Love
Los Angeles; December 13, 1954
(with Ray Anthony & his Orchestra, arr. Dick Reynolds)
Melody of Love
I'm Gonna Live Till I Die
Los Angeles; February 8, 1955
(arr. Nelson Riddle)
Dancing on the Ceiling
Can't We Be Friends?
Glad to Be Unhappy
I'll Be Around
Los Angeles; February 16, 1955
(arr. Nelson Riddle)
What Is This Thing Called Love?
Ill Wind
I See Your Face Before Me
Mood Indigo
Los Angeles; February 17, 1955
(arr. Nelson Riddle)
I Get Along Without You Very Well
In the Wee Small Hours of the Morning
When Your Lover Has Gone
This Love of Mine
Los Angeles; March 4, 1955
(arr. Nelson Riddle)
It Never Entered My Mind
Not as a Stranger
Deep in a Dream
I'll Never Be the Same
Los Angeles; March 7, 1955
If I Had Three Wishes (arr. Nelson Riddle)
How Could You Do a Thing Like That to Me? (arr. Nelson Riddle)

Two Hearts, Two Kisses, with the Nuggets (arr. Dave Cavanaugh)
From the Bottom to the Top, with the Nuggets (arr. Dave Cavanaugh)
Los Angeles; March 23, 1955
Learnin' the Blues (arr. Nelson Riddle)
Los Angeles; July 29, 1955
(arr. Nelson Riddle)
Same Old Saturday Night
Fairy Tale
Los Angeles; August 15, 1955
(arr. Nelson Riddle)
Look To Your Heart, with chorus
Love and Marriage
The Impatient Years
Our Town
Los Angeles; September 13, 1955
(arr. Nelson Riddle)
(Love Is) The Tender Trap
You'll Get Yours
Los Angeles; October 17, 1955
(arr. Nelson Riddle)
You Forgot All the Words
Love Is Here to Stay
Weep They Will
Los Angeles; January 9, 1956
(arr. Nelson Riddle)
You Brought a New Kind of Love to Me
I Thought About You
You Make Me Feel So Young
Memories of You
Los Angeles; January 10, 1956
(arr. Nelson Riddle)
Pennies from Heaven
How About You
You're Getting to Be a Habit with Me
Los Angeles; January 12, 1956
(arr. Nelson Riddle)
It Happened in Monterey
Swingin' Down the Lane
Flowers Mean Forgiveness, with chorus
I've Got You Under My Skin
Los Angeles; January 16, 1956
(arr. Nelson Riddle)
Makin' Whoopee
Old Devil Moon
Anything Goes
Too Marvellous for Words
We'll Be Together Again
Los Angeles; March 8, 1956
(with the Hollywood String Quartet, arr. Nelson Riddle)
Don't Like Goodbyes
P.S. I Love You
Love Locked Out
If It's the Last Thing I Do
Los Angeles; April 4, 1956
(with the Hollywood String Quartet, arr. Nelson Riddle)
I've Had My Moments
Blame It on My Youth
Everything Happens to Me
Wait Till You See Her
Los Angeles; April 5, 1956
(arr. Nelson Riddle)
The End of a Love Affair, with the Hollywood String Quartet
It Could Happen to You, with the Hollywood String Quartet
There's a Flaw in my Flue, with the Hollywood String Quartet

With Every Breath I Take, with the Hollywood String Quartet
How Little We Know
Wait for Me
You're Sensational
Los Angeles; April 9, 1956
(arr. Nelson Riddle)
Five Hundred Guys
Hey Jealous Lover, with chorus
No One Ever Tells You
Los Angeles; April 20, 1956
(with MGM Studio Orchestra, directed by Johnny Green)
You're Sensational (arr. Nelson Riddle)
Who Wants to be a Millionaire, with Celeste Holm (arr. Conrad Salinger)
Mind if I Make Love to You (arr. Nelson Riddle)
Los Angeles; May 7, 1956
Well Did You Evah, with MGM Studio Orchestra & Bing Crosby, directed by Johnny Green (arr. Skip Martin)
Los Angeles; October 1, 1956
(with the Hollywood String Quartet, arr. Nelson Riddle)
I Couldn't Sleep a Wink Last Night
It's Easy to Remember
Close to You
Los Angeles; November 15, 1956
(arr. Nelson Riddle)
I Got Plenty o' Nuttin'
I Won't Dance
Stars Fell on Alabama
Los Angeles; November 20, 1956
(arr. Nelson Riddle)
At Long Last Love
I Guess I'll Have to Change My Plan
I Wish I Were in Love Again
Nice Work if You Can Get It
Los Angeles; November 26, 1956
(arr. Nelson Riddle)
The Lady is a Tramp
Night and Day
The Lonesome Road
If I Had You
Los Angeles; November 28, 1956
(arr. Nelson Riddle)
I Got It Bad and That Ain't Good
From This Moment On
Oh Look at Me Now
You'd Be So Nice to Come Home To
Los Angeles; December 3, 1956
(arr. Nelson Riddle)
Your Love for Me
Can I Steal a Little Love
Los Angeles; March 14, 1957
(arr. Nelson Riddle)
So Long My Love
Crazy Love
Los Angeles; April 10, 1957
(arr. Gordon Jenkins)
Where Is the One
There's No You
The Night We Called It a Day
Autumn Leaves
Los Angeles; April 29, 1957
(arr. Gordon Jenkins)
I Cover the Waterfront
Lonely Town
Laura
Baby Won't You Please Come Home

Los Angeles; May 1, 1957
(arr. Gordon Jenkins)
Where Are You
I Think of You
I'm a Fool to Want You
Maybe You'll Be There
Los Angeles; May 20, 1957
(arr. Nelson Riddle)
Witchcraft
Something Wonderful Happens in Summer
Tell Her You Love Her
You're Cheatin' Yourself (If You're Cheatin' on Me)
Los Angeles; July 10, 1957
(with the Ralph Brewster Singers, arr. Gordon Jenkins)
It Came Upon a Midnight Clear
O Little Town of Bethlehem
Hark the Herald Angels Sing
Adeste Fideles (O Come All Ye Faithful)
Los Angeles; July 16, 1957
(with the Ralph Brewster Singers, arr. Gordon Jenkins)
Jingle Bells
The First Noel
Have Yourself a Merry Little Christmas
The Christmas Waltz
Los Angeles; July 17, 1957
(with the Ralph Brewster Singers, arr. Gordon Jenkins)
Mistletoe and Holly
The Christmas Song
Silent Night
I'll Be Home for Christmas
Los Angeles; August 13, 1957
I Could Write a Book, orchestra directed by Morris Stoloff (arr. Nelson Riddle)
Bewitched, orchestra directed by Morris Stoloff (arr. Nelson Riddle)
All the Way, orchestra directed by Nelson Riddle (arr. Nelson Riddle)
There's a Small Hotel, directed by Morris Stoloff (arr. Nelson Riddle)
Chicago, orchestra directed by Nelson Riddle (arr. Nelson Riddle)
Los Angeles; September 25, 1957
(orchestra directed by Morris Stoloff, arr. Nelson Riddle)
I Didn't Know What Time It Was
What Do I Care for a Dame
Los Angeles; October 1, 1957
(arr. Billy May)
On the Road to Mandalay
Let's Get Away from It All
Isle of Capri
Los Angeles; October 3, 1957
(arr. Billy May)
Autumn in New York
London by Night
April in Paris
Moonlight in Vermont
Los Angeles; October 8, 1957
(arr. Billy May)
Blue Hawaii
Come Fly with Me
Around the World
It's Nice to Go Trav'ling
Brazil

Los Angeles; November 25, 1957
(arr. Nelson Riddle)
I Believe
Everybody Loves Somebody
It's the Same Old Dream
Time After Time
Los Angeles; December 11, 1957
(arr. Nelson Riddle)
You'll Always Be the One I Love
If You Are But a Dream
Put Your Dreams Away
Los Angeles; March 3, 1958
(arr. Billy May)
Nothing in Common, with Keely Smith
How Are Ya Fixed for Love, with Keely Smith
Same Old Song and Dance
Los Angeles; May 29, 1958
(orchestra directed by Felix Slatkin)
Monique (arr. Felix Slatkin)
Ebb Tide (arr. Nelson Riddle)
Angel Eyes (arr. Nelson Riddle)
Spring is Here (arr. Nelson Riddle)
Guess I'll Hang My Tears Out to Dry (arr. Nelson Riddle)
Only the Lonely (arr. Nelson Riddle)
Willow Weep for Me (arr. Nelson Riddle)
Los Angeles; June 24, 1958
(arr. Nelson Riddle)
Blues in the Night
What's New
Gone with the Wind
Los Angeles; June 25, 1958
(arr. Nelson Riddle)
Goodbye
It's a Lonesome Old Town
One for My Baby, with piano solo by Bill Miller
Los Angeles; September 11, 1958
(arr. Nelson Riddle)
Mr. Success
Sleep Warm
Where or When
Los Angeles; September 30, 1958
It All Depends on You (arr. Billy May)
Los Angeles; October 1, 1958
I Couldn't Care Less (arr. Nelson Riddle)
Los Angeles; October 28, 1958
To Love and Be Loved (arr. Nelson Riddle)
Los Angeles; December 5, 1958
To Love and Be Loved (arr. Nelson Riddle)
Los Angeles; December 9, 1958
(arr. Billy May)
The Song Is You
Something's Gotta Give
Just in Time
Los Angeles; December 22, 1958
Day In, Day Out (arr. Billy May)
Baubles, Bangles, and Beads (arr. Billy May)
Dancing in the Dark (arr. Billy May)
Saturday Night (arr. Heinie Beau)
Cheek to Cheek (arr. Billy May)
Los Angeles; December 23, 1958
(orchestra directed by Billy May)
Too Close for Comfort (arr. Heinie Beau)

I Could Have Danced All Night (arr. Billy May)
Come Dance with Me (arr. Billy May)
The Last Dance (arr. Heinie Beau)
Los Angeles; December 29, 1958
(arr. Nelson Riddle)
The Moon Was Yellow
They Came to Cordura
All My Tomorrows
French Foreign Legion
Los Angeles; March 24, 1959
(arr. Gordon Jenkins)
A Ghost of a Chance
Why Try to Change Me Now
None But the Lonely Heart
Stormy Weather
Los Angeles; March 25, 1959
(arr. Gordon Jenkins)
Here's That Rainy Day
The One I Love Belongs to Someone Else
Los Angeles; March 26, 1959
(arr. Gordon Jenkins)
I Can't Get Started
Where Do You Go
A Cottage for Sale
Just Friends
Los Angeles; May 8, 1959
(arr. Nelson Riddle)
High Hopes, with Eddie Hodges & A Bunch of Kids
Love Looks So Well on You
Los Angeles; May 14, 1959
This Was My Love
Talk to Me (arr. Nelson Riddle)
When No One Cares (arr. Gordon Jenkins)
I'll Never Smile Again (arr. Gordon Jenkins)
Los Angeles; February 19, 1960
(arr. Nelson Riddle)
It's All Right with Me
C'est Magnifique
I Love Paris, with Maurice Chevalier
Los Angeles; February 20, 1960
(arr. Nelson Riddle)
Let's Do It, with Shirley MacLaine
Montmart', with Maurice Chevalier & chorus
Los Angeles; March 1, 1960
(arr. Nelson Riddle)
You Go to My Head
Fools Rush In
That Old Feeling
Try a Little Tenderness
Los Angeles; March 2, 1960
(arr. Nelson Riddle)
She's Funny That Way
The Nearness of You
Nevertheless
Los Angeles; March 3, 1960
(arr. Nelson Riddle)
Dream
I've Got a Crush on You
Embraceable You
Mam'selle
How Deep is the Ocean
Los Angeles; April 12, 1960
(arr. Nelson Riddle)
Nice 'n' Easy
River Stay 'Way from My Door
I Love Paris

It's Over, It's Over, It's Over, with chorus
Los Angeles; August 22, 1960
(arr. Nelson Riddle)
When You're Smiling
I Concentrate on You
You Do Something to Me
S'posin'
Should I
Los Angeles; August 23, 1960
(arr. Nelson Riddle)
My Blue Heaven
I Can't Believe That You're in Love with Me
Always
It All Depends on You
Los Angeles; August 31, 1960
(arr. Nelson Riddle)
It's Only a Paper Moon
September in the Rain
Hidden Persuasion
Los Angeles; September 1, 1960
(arr. Nelson Riddle)
Sentimental Baby
Ol' MacDonald
Blue Moon
Los Angeles; March 20, 1961
(orchestra directed by Billy May)
On the Sunny Side of the Street (arr. Heinie Beau)
Day by Day (arr. Billy May)
Sentimental Journey (arr. Heinie Beau)
Don't Take Your Love from Me (arr. Heinie Beau)
Los Angeles; March 21, 1961
(orchestra directed by Billy May)
Yes Indeed (arr. Billy May)
American Beauty Rose (arr. Heinie Beau)
I've Heard That Song Before (arr. Billy May)
That Old Black Magic (arr. Heinie Beau)
Los Angeles; March 22, 1961
Five Minutes More (arr. Billy May)
Almost Like Being in Love (arr. Billy May)
Lover (arr. Heinie Beau)
Paper Doll (arr. Billy May)
Los Angeles; September 11, 1961
(arr. Axel Stordahl)
I'll Be Seeing You
I'll See You Again
September Song
Memories of You
There Will Never Be Another You
When the World Was Young
Los Angeles; September 12, 1961
Somewhere Along the Way (arr. Axel Stordahl)
A Million Dreams Ago (arr. Axel Stordahl)
These Foolish Things (arr. Axel Stordahl)
As Time Goes By (arr. Axel Stordahl)
It's a Blue World (arr. Heinie Beau)
I'll Remember April (arr. Heinie Beau)
Los Angeles; March 6, 1962
I Gotta Right to Sing the Blues (arr. Skip Martin)

The Reprise Years: 1960–1983

Los Angeles; December 19, 1960
(arr. Johnny Mandel)
Ring-A-Ding-Ding
Let's Fall in Love
In the Still of the Night
A Foggy Day
Let's Face the Music and Dance
You'd Be So Easy to Love
A Fine Romance
Los Angeles; December 20, 1960
(arr. Johnny Mandel)
The Coffee Song
Be Careful It's My Heart
I've Got My Love to Keep Me Warm
You and the Night and the Music
When I Take My Sugar to Tea
Los Angeles; December 21, 1960
(arr. Felix Slatkin)
The Second Time Around
Tina
Los Angeles; May 1, 1961
(arr. Sy Oliver)
I'll Be Seeing You
I'm Getting Sentimental Over You
Imagination
Take Me
Los Angeles; May 2, 1961
(arr. Sy Oliver)
Without a Song
Polka Dots and Moonbeams
Daybreak
Los Angeles; May 3, 1961
(arr. Sy Oliver)
The One I Love Belongs to Somebody Else, with Sy Oliver
There Are Such Things
It's Always You
It Started All Over Again
East of the Sun
Los Angeles; May 18, 1961
(arr. Billy May)
The Curse of an Aching Heart
Love Walked In
Please Don't Talk About Me When I'm Gone
Have You Met Miss Jones
Los Angeles; May 19, 1961
(arr. Billy May)
Don't Be That Way
I Never Knew
Falling in Love with Love
It's a Wonderful World
Los Angeles; May 23, 1961
(arr. Billy May)
Don't Cry Joe
You're Nobody Till Somebody Loves You
Moonlight on the Ganges
Granada
Hollywood; November 20, 1961
(arr. Don Costa)
Stardust
Yesterdays
I Hadn't Anyone Till You
Hollywood; November 21, 1961
(arr. Don Costa)
It Might as Well Be Spring
Prisoner of Love
That's All

Don't Take Your Love from Me
Misty
Hollywood; November 22, 1961
Come Rain or Come Shine (arr. Don Costa)
Night and Day (arr. Don Costa)
All or Nothing at All (arr. Don Costa)
Pocketful of Miracles (arr. Nelson Riddle)
Name It and It's Yours (arr. Nelson Riddle)
Los Angeles; January 15, 1962
(arr. Gordon Jenkins)
The Song Is Ended
All Alone
Charmaine
When I Lost You
Los Angeles; January 16, 1962
(arr. Gordon Jenkins)
Remember
Together
The Girl Next Door
Indiscreet
Los Angeles; January 17, 1962
(arr. Gordon Jenkins)
What'll I Do
Oh How I Miss You Tonight
Are You Lonesome Tonight
Los Angeles; February 27, 1962
(arr. Neal Hefti)
Everybody's Twistin'
Nothing But the Best
Hollywood; April 10, 1962
(arr. Neal Hefti)
I'm Beginning to See the Light
I Get a Kick Out of You
Ain't She Sweet
I Love You
They Can't Take That Away from Me
Love is Just Around the Corner
Hollywood; April 11, 1962
(arr. Neal Hefti)
At Long Last Love
Serenade in Blue
Goody, Goody
Don'cha Go 'Way Mad
Tangerine
Pick Yourself Up
London; June 12, 1962
(arr. Robert Farnon)
If I Had You
The Very Thought of You
I'll Follow My Secret Heart
A Garden in the Rain
London; June 13, 1962
(arr. Robert Farnon)
London by Night
The Gypsy
A Nightingale Sang in Berkeley Square
London; June 14, 1962
(arr. Robert Farnon)
We'll Meet Again
Now Is the Hour
We'll Gather Lilacs
Los Angeles; August 27, 1962
(orchestra directed by Neal Hefti, arr. Nelson Riddle)
The Look of Love
I Left My Heart in San Francisco
Los Angeles; October 2, 1962
(with Count Basie & His Orchestra, arr. Neal Hefti)

Nice Work if You Can Get It
Please Be Kind
I Won't Dance
Learnin' the Blues
Los Angeles; October 3, 1962
(with Count Basie & His Orchestra, arr. Neal Hefti)
I'm Gonna Sit Right Down and Write Myself a Letter
I Only Have Eyes for You
My Kind of Girl
Pennies from Heaven
The Tender Trap
Looking at the World Through Rose Colored Glasses
Los Angeles; October 22, 1962
Me and My Shadow, with Sammy Davis Jr. (arr. Billy May)
Los Angeles; January 21, 1963
(arr. Nelson Riddle)
Come Blow Your Horn
Call Me Irresponsible
Hollywood; February 18, 1963
(arr. Nelson Riddle)
Lost in the Stars
My Heart Stood Still
Ol' Man River
Hollywood; February 19, 1963
(arr. Nelson Riddle)
This Nearly Was Mine
You'll Never Walk Alone
I Have Dreamed
Hollywood; February 20, 1963
Bewitched (arr. Nelson Riddle)
Hollywood; February 21, 1963
Soliloquy (arr. Nelson Riddle)
You Brought a New Kind of Love to Me (arr. Nelson Riddle)
Los Angeles; April 29, 1963
(arr. Nelson Riddle)
In the Wee Small Hours of the Morning
Nancy
Young at Heart
The Second Time Around
All the Way
Los Angeles; April 30, 1963
(arr. Nelson Riddle)
Witchcraft
How Little We Know
Put Your Dreams Away
I've Got You Under My Skin
Oh What It Seemed to Be
Los Angeles; July 10, 1963
(orchestra directed by Morris Stoloff)
We Open in Venice, with Sammy Davis Jr. and Dean Martin (arr. Billy May)
Guys and Dolls, with Dean Martin (arr. Bill Loose)
Los Angeles; July 18, 1963
(orchestra directed by Morris Stoloff, arr. Nelson Riddle)
Old Devil Moon
When I'm Not Near the Girl I Love
I've Never Been in Love Before
Los Angeles; July 24, 1963
(orchestra directed by Morris Stoloff)
So in Love, with Keely Smith (arr. Nelson Riddle)
Some Enchanted Evening, with Rosemary Clooney (arr. Nelson Riddle)

Luck Be a Lady (arr. Billy May)
Guys and Dolls (reprise), with Dean Martin (arr. Bill Loose)
Los Angeles; July 29, 1963
(orchestra directed by Morris Stoloff)
Fugue for Tinhorns, with Bing Crosby & Dean Martin (arr. Bill Loose)
The Oldest Established (Permanent Floating Crap Game in New York), with Bing Crosby & Dean Martin (arr. Billy May)
Los Angeles; July 31, 1963
Some Enchanted Evening, orchestra directed by Morris Stoloff (arr. Nelson Riddle)
Twin Soliloquies (Wonder How It Feels), with Keely Smith & orchestra directed by Morris Stoloff (arr. Nelson Riddle)
Here's to Losers, orchestra directed by Marty Paich (arr. Marty Paich)
Love Isn't Just for the Young, orchestra directed by Marty Paich (arr. Marty Paich)
Los Angeles; October 13, 1963
Have Yourself a Merry Little Christmas, orchestra & chorus directed by Gus Levene (arr. Gil Frau)
Los Angeles; December 3, 1963
(arr. Don Costa)
Talk to Me Baby
Stay with Me (main theme from *The Cardinal*)
Los Angeles; January 2, 1964
(with Fred Waring & His Pennsylvanians)
You're a Lucky Fellow Mr. Smith (arr. Jack Halloran)
The House I Live In (arr. Nelson Riddle)
Early American (arr. Nelson Riddle)
Los Angeles; January 27, 1964
(arr. Nelson Riddle)
The Way You Look Tonight
Three Coins in the Fountain
Swinging on a Star
In the Cool, Cool, Cool of the Evening
The Continental
Los Angeles; January 28, 1964
(arr. Nelson Riddle)
It Might as Well Be Spring
Secret Love
Moon River
Days of Wine and Roses
Love is a Many Splendoured Thing
Los Angeles; February 4, 1964
(with Fred Waring & His Pennsylvanians and Bing Crosby)
Let us Break Bread Together (arr. Roy Ringwald)
You Never Had It So Good (arr. Jack Halloran)
Los Angeles; April 8, 1964
(arr. Nelson Riddle)
My Kind of Town
I Like to Lead When I Dance
I Can't Believe I'm Losing You, overdubbed with guitar on March 15, 1968, and released as a single (arr. Don Costa)
Los Angeles; April 10, 1964
(arr. Nelson Riddle)

Style, with Bing Crosby & Dean Martin
Mister Booze, with Bing Crosby, Dean Martin, Sammy Davis Jr. & chorus
Don't Be a Do-Badder, with Bing Crosby, Dean Martin, Sammy Davis Jr. & chorus
Los Angeles; June 9, 1964
(with Count Basie & His Orchestra, arr. Quincy Jones)
The Best Is Yet to Come
I Wanna Be Around
I Believe in You
Fly Me to the Moon
Los Angeles; June 10, 1964
(with Count Basie & His Orchestra, arr. Quincy Jones)
Hello Dolly
The Good Life
I Wish You Love
Los Angeles; June 12, 1964
(with Count Basie & His Orchestra, arr. Quincy Jones)
I Can't Stop Loving You
More
Wives and Lovers
Los Angeles; June 16, 1964
(with Fred Waring & His Pennsylvanians)
An Old Fashioned Christmas (arr. Nelson Riddle)
I Heard the Bells on Christmas Day (arr. Nelson Riddle)
The Little Drummer Boy (arr. Dick Reynolds)
Los Angeles; June 19, 1964
(with Fred Waring & His Pennsylvanians, arr. Jack Halloran)
Go Tell it on the Mountain, with Bing Crosby
We Wish You the Merriest, with Bing Crosby (co-arr. Harry Betts)
Los Angeles; July 17, 1964
(with chorus)
Softly as I Leave You (arr. Ernie Freeman)
Then Suddenly Love (arr. Ernie Freeman)
Since Marie Has Left Paree (arr. Billy May)
Available (arr. Ernie Freeman)
Los Angeles; October 3, 1964
(with chorus)
Pass Me By (arr. Billy May)
Emily (arr. Nelson Riddle)
Dear Heart (arr. Nelson Riddle)
Los Angeles; November 11, 1964
(with vocal chorus, arr. Ernie Freeman)
Somewhere in Your Heart
Anytime at All
Hollywood; April 13, 1965
(arr. Gordon Jenkins)
Don't Wait Too Long
September Song
Last Night When We Were Young
Hello Young Lovers
Hollywood; April 14, 1965
I See It Now (arr. Gordon Jenkins)
When the Wind Was Green (arr. Gordon Jenkins)

Once Upon a Time (arr. Gordon Jenkins)
How Old Am I (arr. Gordon Jenkins)
Tell Her You Love Her Each Day, with chorus (arr. Ernie Freeman)
When Somebody Loves You, with chorus (arr. Ernie Freeman)
Hollywood; April 22, 1965
(arr. Gordon Jenkins)
It Was a Very Good Year
The Man in the Looking Glass
This is All I Ask
It Gets Lonely Early
How Old Am I, overdubbed with guitar on March 15, 1968, and released as a single
Los Angeles; May 6, 1965
Forget Domani (arr. Ernie Freeman)
Hollywood; May 27, 1965
The September of My Years (arr. Gordon Jenkins)
Hollywood; August 23, 1965
(arr. Torrie Zito)
Everybody Has the Right to Be Wrong! (At Least Once)
I'll Only Miss Her When I Think of Her
Golden Moment (arr. Nelson Riddle)
Hollywood; October 11, 1965
(with orchestra directed by Sonny Burke)
Come Fly with Me (arr. Billy May)
I'll Never Smile Again, with chorus (arr. Freddy Stultz)
Hollywood; October 21, 1965
(arr. Nelson Riddle)
Moment to Moment (orchestral track recorded September 14, 1965)
Love and Marriage (orchestral track recorded October 11, 1965)
Hollywood; November 29, 1965
(arr. Nelson Riddle)
Moon Song
Moon Love
The Moon Got in My Eyes
Moonlight Serenade
Reaching for the Moon
Hollywood; November 30, 1965
(arr. Nelson Riddle)
I Wished on the Moon
Moonlight Becomes You
Moonlight Mood
Oh You Crazy Moon
The Moon Was Yellow
Las Vegas; January 26–February 1, 1966
(two shows each night; with Count Basie & His Orchestra, arr. Quincy Jones)
I've Got a Crush on You
I've Got You Under My Skin
The September of My Years
Street of Dreams
You Make Me Feel So Young
The Shadow of Your Smile
Luck Be a Lady
It Was a Very Good Year
Don't Worry 'Bout Me
My Kind of Town
One for My Baby
Fly Me to the Moon
Get Me to the Church on Time
Angel Eyes

Where or When
Come Fly with Me
Hollywood; April 11, 1966
Strangers in the Night (arr. Ernie
  Freeman)
Hollywood; May 11, 1966
(arr. Nelson Riddle)
My Baby Just Cares for Me
Yes Sir, That's My Baby
You're Driving Me Crazy
The Most Beautiful Girl in the World
Hollywood; May 16, 1966
(Nelson Riddle)
Summer Wind
All or Nothing at All
Call Me
*On a Clear Day (You Can See
  Forever)*
Downtown
Hollywood; October 18, 1966
That's Life (arr. Ernie Freeman)
Hollywood; November 17, 1966
(arr. Ernie Freeman)
Give Her Love
What Now My Love
Somewhere My Love
Winchester Cathedral
Hollywood; November 18, 1966
(arr. Ernie Freeman)
I Will Wait for You
You're Gonna Hear from Me
Sand and Sea
The Impossible Dream
Hollywood; January 30, 1967
(arr. Claus Ogerman)
Baubles, Bangles, and Beads, with
  Antonio Carlos Jobim
I Concentrate on You, with Antonio
  Carlos Jobim
Dindi
Change Partners
Hollywood; January 31, 1967
(arr. Claus Ogerman)
*Quiet Nights of Quiet Stars
  (Corcovado)*
If You Never Come to Me
The Girl From Ipanema, with
  Antonio Carlos Jobim
Meditation
Hollywood; February 1, 1967
Once I Loved (arr. Claus Ogerman)
How Insensitive, with Antonio Carlos
  Jobim (arr. Claus Ogerman)
Drinking Again (arr. Claus Ogerman)
Somethin' Stupid, with Nancy Sinatra
  (arr. Billy Strange)
New York City; June 29, 1967
You Are There (arr. Gordon Jenkins)
The World We Knew (arr. Ernie
  Freeman)
Hollywood; July 24, 1967
Born Free (arr. Gordon Jenkins)
This Is My Love (arr. Gordon
  Jenkins)
This Is My Song (arr. Ernie Freeman)
Don't Sleep in the Subway, with
  chorus (arr. Ernie Freeman)
Some Enchanted Evening (arr. H.B.
  Barnum)
This Town (arr. Billy Strange)
Hollywood; September 20, 1967
Younger than Springtime (arr. Billy
  Strange)

Hollywood; December 11, 1967
(with Duke Ellington & His
  Orchestra, arr. Billy May)
All I Need Is the Girl
Yellow Days
Indian Summer
Come Back to Me
Hollywood; December 12, 1967
(with Duke Ellington & His
  Orchestra, arr. Billy May)
Sunny
Follow Me
I Like the Sunrise
Poor Butterfly
New York City; July 24, 1968
(arr. Don Costa)
My Way of Life
Cycles
Whatever Happened to Christmas
Hollywood; August 12, 1968
(arr. Nelson Riddle)
The Twelve Days of Christmas, with
  Frank Sinatra Jr., Nancy Sinatra,
  and Tina Sinatra
*The Bells of Christmas
  (Greensleeves),* with Frank Sinatra
  Jr., Nancy Sinatra, and Tina
  Sinatra
I Wouldn't Trade Christmas, with
  Frank Sinatra Jr., Nancy Sinatra,
  and Tina Sinatra
The Christmas Waltz
Hollywood; November 11, 1968
(arr. Nelson Riddle)
Blue Lace
Star
Hollywood; November 12, 1968
(orchestra directed by Bill Miller,
  arr. Don Costa)
Little Green Apples
Gentle on my Mind
By the Time I Get to Phoenix
Hollywood; November 13, 1968
(orchestra directed by Bill Miller,
  arr. Don Costa)
Moody River
Pretty Colours
Hollywood; November 14, 1968
(orchestra directed by Bill Miller,
  arr. Don Costa)
Rain in my Heart
Wandering
From Both Sides Now
Hollywood; December 30, 1968
My Way (arr. Don Costa)
Hollywood; February 11, 1969
(orchestra directed by Morris Stoloff,
  arr. Eumir Deodato)
One Note Samba, with Antonio Carlos
  Jobim
Don't Ever Go Away
Wave
Bonita
Hollywood; February 12, 1969
(orchestra directed by Morris Stoloff,
  arr. Eumir Deodato)
Someone to Light up My Life
Drinking Water (Aqua De Beber),
  with Antonio Carlos Jobim
Hollywood; February 13, 1969
(orchestra directed by Morris Stoloff)
Song of the Sabia (arr. Eumir
  Deodato)

This Happy Madness, with Antonio
  Carlos Jobim (arr. Eumir Deodato)
Triste (arr. Eumir Deodato)
All My Tomorrows (arr. Don Costa)
Didn't We (arr. Don Costa)
Hollywood; February 20, 1969
(arr. Don Costa)
A Day in the Life of a Fool
Yesterday
If You Go Away
Hollywood; February 24, 1969
(arr. Don Costa)
Watch What Happens
For Once in my Life
Mrs. Robinson
Hallelujah, I Love Her So
Hollywood; February 25, 1969
Shadow of the Moon (arr. Don Costa)
Hollywood; March 19, 1969
(arr. Don Costa)
I've Been to Town
Empty Is
The Single Man
Lonesome Cities
Hollywood; March 20, 1969
(arr. Don Costa)
The Beautiful Strangers
A Man Alone
A Man Alone (reprise)
Love's Been Good to Me
Hollywood; March 21, 1969
(arr. Don Costa)
Out Beyond the Window
Night
Some Travelling Music
From Promise to Promise
New York City; July 14, 1969
(arr. Joseph Scott & Bob Gaudio)
I Would Be in Love (Anyway)
The Train
Goodbye
New York City; July 15, 1969
(arr. Charles Calello)
Watertown
Elizabeth
Michael and Peter
New York City; July 16, 1969
(arr. Joseph Scott & Bob Gaudio)
She Says, with chorus
What's Now Is Now
New York City; July 17, 1969
(arr. Charles Calello)
For a While
What a Funny Girl (You Used to Be)
New York City; August 18, 1969
(arr. Don Costa)
Forget to Remember
Goin' Out of My Head
Hollywood; November 7, 1969
Lady Day (arr. Don Costa)
Hollywood; October 26, 1970
(arr. Don Costa)
I Will Drink the Wine
Bein' Green
My Sweet Lady
Hollywood; October 27, 1970
Sunrise in the Morning (arr. Don
  Costa)
Hollywood; October 28, 1970
(arr. Lenny Hayton)
I'm Not Afraid
Something

Hollywood; October 29, 1970
(arr. Don Costa)
Leaving on a Jet Plane
Close to You
Hollywood; November 2, 1970
(arr. Don Costa)
Feelin' Kinda Sunday, with Nancy
  Sinatra
Life's a Trippy Thing, with Nancy
  Sinatra
Hollywood; June 4, 1973
(arr. Gordon Jenkins)
You Will Be My Music
Noah, with chorus
Hollywood; June 5, 1973
(arr. Gordon Jenkins)
Nobody Wins
The Hurt Doesn't Go Away
Hollywood; June 21, 1973
(orchestra directed by Gordon
  Jenkins, arr. Don Costa)
Winners
Let Me Try Again
Hollywood; June 22, 1973
(arr. Gordon Jenkins)
Empty Tables
Walk Away
Send in the Clowns
There Used to Be a Ballpark
Hollywood; August 20, 1973
(orchestra directed by Gordon
  Jenkins)
*You're So Right (For What's Wrong in
  My Life)* (arr. Gordon Jenkins)
Dream Away (arr. Don Costa)
Hollywood; December 10, 1973
(arr. Don Costa)
Bad, Bad Leroy Brown
I'm Gonna Make It All the Way
Hollywood; May 7, 1974
(arr. Gordon Jenkins)
If
The Summer Knows
Hollywood; May 8, 1974
(arr. Don Costa)
Sweet Caroline
You Turned My World Around
Hollywood; May 21, 1974
(arr. Don Costa)
*What Are You Doing the Rest of Your
  Life*
*Tie a Yellow Ribbon Round the Ole
  Oak Tree*
Satisfy Me One More Time
Hollywood; May 24, 1974
(arr. Don Costa)
You Are the Sunshine of My Life
  (orchestral track recorded May 21,
  1974)
New York City; October 13, 1974
(orchestra directed by Bill Miller,
  with Woody Herman & the Young
  Thundering Herd)
The Lady Is a Tramp (arr. Billy
  Byers)
I Get a Kick Out of You (arr. Nelson
  Riddle)
Let Me Try Again (arr. Don Costa)
Autumn in New York (arr. Billy May)
I've Got You Under My Skin (arr.
  Nelson Riddle)
Bad, Bad Leroy Brown (arr. Don
  Costa)

Angel Eyes (arr. Nelson Riddle)
You Are the Sunshine of My Life
  (arr. Nelson Riddle)
The House I Live In (arr. Nelson
  Riddle)
My Kind of Town (arr. Nelson Riddle)
My Way (arr. Don Costa)
Hollywood; March 3, 1975
(with chorus, orchestra directed by
  Bill Miller)
Anytime (I'll Be There) (arr. Don
  Costa)
The Only Couple on the Floor
  (arr. Don Costa)
I Believe I'm Gonna Love You
  (arr. Al Capps)
New York City; August 18, 1975
The Saddest Thing of All (arr. Gordon
  Jenkins; orchestral track recorded
  August 4, 1975)
Hollywood; October 24, 1975
(arr. Don Costa)
A Baby Just Like You, with chorus
Christmas Mem'ries, with chorus
Hollywood; February 5, 1976
(orchestra directed by Bill Miller,
  arr. Don Costa)
I Sing the Songs (I Write the Songs)
Empty Tables, with Bill Miller on
  piano
Send in the Clowns, with Bill Miller
  on piano
Hollywood; June 21, 1976
(saxophone solos by Sam Butera)
The Best I Ever Had (arr. Billy May)
Stargazer, Orchestra directed by Bill
  Miller (arr. Don Costa)
New York City; September 27, 1976
Dry Your Eyes, orchestra directed
  by Bill Miller (arr. Don Costa;
  orchestral track recorded June 21
  in Hollywood)
Like a Sad Song (arr. Claus
  Ogerman)
Hollywood; November 12, 1976
I Love My Wife (arr. Nelson Riddle)
New York City; February 16, 1977
(orchestral tracks recorded
  February 15)
Night and Day (arr. Joe Beck)
Everybody Ought to Be in Love
  (arr. Charles Calello)
Los Angeles; July 18, 1979
(arr. Billy May)
I Had the Craziest Dream, with
  chorus
It Had to Be You
New York City; August 20, 1979
(arr. Don Costa)
You & Me
Summer Me, Winter Me
McArthur Park
New York City; August 21, 1979
(arr. Don Costa)
For the Good Times, with Eileen
  Farrell & chorus
What God Looks Like to Me
Love Me Tender, with chorus
New York City; August 22, 1979
(arr. Don Costa)
Just the Way You Are
Song Sung Blue, with chorus

Los Angeles; September 17, 1979
(arr. Billy May)
All of You
My Shining Hour, with chorus
More than You Know, with chorus
Los Angeles; September 18, 1979
(arr. Billy May)
The Song is You
But Not for Me, with chorus
Street of Dreams
They All Laughed
Los Angeles; September 19, 1979
Let's Face the Music and Dance,
orchestra conducted by Vinnie
Falcone (arr. Don Costa)
New York, New York (arr. Billy May)
Los Angeles; December 3, 1979
Something, orchestra conducted by
Vinnie Falcone (arr. Nelson
Riddle)
Los Angeles; December 17, 1979
(with chorus and Los Angeles
Philharmonic Symphony
Orchestra, arr. Gordon Jenkins)
The Future
I've Been There
Song Without Words
Los Angeles; December 18, 1979
(with chorus and Los Angeles
Philharmonic Symphony
Orchestra, arr. Gordon Jenkins)
Before the Music Ends
*What Time Does the Next Miracle
Leave*
World War None
Hollywood; April 8, 1981
(arr. and conducted Gordon Jenkins)
Bang, Bang
*The Gal That Got Away/It Never
Entered My Mind*
New York City; July 20, 1981
(arr. and conducted Gordon Jenkins)
Thanks for the Memory
I Love Her
A Long Night
New York City; July 21, 1981 (day)
Say Hello (arr. and conducted Don
Costa)
New York City; July 21, 1981 (night)
South to a Warmer Place (arr. and
conducted Gordon Jenkins)
New York City; August 19, 1981
Good Thing Going (arr. and conduct-
ed Don Costa)
New York City; September 10, 1981
(arr. and conducted Gordon Jenkins)
Monday Morning Quarterback
Hey Look, No Crying (edited version
released)
Los Angeles; February 28, 1983
It's Sunday (guitar arrangement
played by Tony Mottola)
Location(s) unknown; late 1983–1984
L.A. Is My Lady
The Best of Everything
How Do You Keep the Music Playing?
Teach Me Tonight
It's All Right with Me
Mack the Knife
Until the Real Thing Comes Along
Stormy Weather
If I Should Lose You
A Hundred Years from Today
After You're Gone

* specific dates and locations for each
session not available; these songs
make up the album *L.A. Is My
Lady,* released in 1984 on Quest
Records.
**Boston, Detroit, Dublin, Hollywood,
London, Los Angeles, Miami, New
York City, Rio de Janeiro, Studio
City (California); various dates,
early 1993***
(musical director and conductor,
Patrick Williams; pianist for
Sinatra, Bill Miller)
The Lady Is a Tramp, with Luther
Vandross
What Now My Love, with Aretha
Franklin
I've Got a Crush on You, with Barbra
Streisand
Summer Wind, with Julio Iglesias
Come Rain or Come Shine, with
Gloria Estefan
New York, New York, with Tony
Bennett
They Can't Take That Away from Me,
with Natalie Cole
You Make Me Feel So Young, with
Charles Aznavour
*Guess I'll Hang My Tears Out to
Dry/In the Wee Small Hours of the
Morning,* with Carly Simon
I've Got the World on a String, with
Liza Minelli
Witchcraft, with Anita Baker
I've Got You Under My Skin, with
Bono
*All the Way/One for My Baby (and
One More for the Road),* with
Kenny G
* specific dates and locations for each
session not available; for some
songs, the vocal tracks were
recorded in separate locations and
later mixed to create the final
product: the first *Duets* album.
**Austin, Bedford (New York),
Hollywood, London, Los Angeles,
Mexico City, Miami, Nashville, New
York City, San Rafael (California),
Rio de Janeiro; early 1994***
(musical director and conductor,
Patrick Williams; pianist for
Sinatra, Bill Miller)
For Once in My Life, with Gladys
Knight & Stevie Wonder; piano,
harmonica & vocal ad lib by Stevie
Wonder (arr. Don Costa)
Come Fly with Me, with Luis Miguel
(arr. Billy May)
Bewitched, with Patti Labelle (arr.
Patrick Williams)
The Best Is Yet to Come, with Jon
Secada (arr. Quincy Jones)
Moonlight in Vermont, with Linda
Ronstadt (arr. Patrick Williams)
Fly Me to the Moon, with Antonio
Carlos Jobim; introduction per-
formed by Antonio Carlos Jobim
et al (arr. Quincy Jones & Patrick
Williams)
Luck Be a Lady, with Chrissie Hynde
(arr. Billy May)
A Foggy Day, with Willie Nelson
(arr. Johnny Mandel)

Where or When, with Steve Lawrence
and Eydie Gorme (arr. Bill Byers)
Embraceable You, with Lena Horne
(arr. Nelson Riddle)
Mack the Knife, with Jimmy Buffett
(arr. Frank Foster & Patrick
Williams)
*How Do You Keep the Music
Playing?/My Funny Valentine,*
with Lorrie Morgan (arr. Patrick
Williams)
*The House I Live In (That's America
to Me),* with Neil Diamond (arr.
Don Costa; vocal arr. Tom Hensley
& Alan Lindgren)
* specific dates and locations for each
session not available; for some
songs, the vocal tracks were
recorded in separate locations and
later mixed to create the final
product: the second *Duets* album.

Filmography

***indicates a musical or a film in which
Sinatra sang as well as acted**
*Las Vegas Nights** (Paramount, 1941).
Appeared as male vocalist with
Tommy Dorsey Orchestra.
*Ships Ahoy** (Metro-Goldwyn-Mayer,
1942). Appeared as male vocalist with
the Tommy Dorsey Orchestra.
*Reveille with Beverly** (Columbia,
1943). Appeared as solo performer.
*Higher and Higher** (RKO, 1943). In his
first starring role, opposite Michele
Morgan.
*Step Lively** (RKO, 1943). Appeared
opposite Gloria de Haven.
*Anchors Aweigh** (Metro-Goldwyn-
Mayer, 1945). Starred opposite
Kathryn Grayson & Gene Kelly.
*The House I Live In** (RKO, 1945).
Starring role in this plea for racial
tolerance.
*Till the Clouds Roll By** (Metro-Goldwyn-
Mayer, 1946). Guest-starred in this bio
pic of composer Jerome Kern.
*It Happened in Brooklyn** (Metro-
Goldwyn-Mayer, 1947). Starred
opposite Kathryn Grayson.
*The Miracle of the Bells** (RKO, 1948).
Dramatic role as a Catholic priest.
*The Kissing Bandit** (Metro-Goldwyn-
Mayer, 1948). Starred opposite
Kathryn Grayson.
*Take Me Out to the Ball Game** (MGM,
1949). Starred opposite Esther
Williams & Gene Kelly.
*On the Town** (MGM, 1949). Starred
opposite Gene Kelly.
*Double Dynamite** (RKO Radio, 1951).
Starred with Jane Russell & Groucho
Marx.
*Meet Danny Wilson** (Universal-
International, 1951). Starred with
Shelley Winters & Alex Nicol.
From Here to Eternity (Columbia,
1953). Starred with Burt Lancaster,

Montgomery Clift, Deborah Kern &
Donna Reed.
Suddenly (Libra Production/United
Artists Release, 1954). Starred with
Sterling Hayden, James Gleason &
Nancy Gates.
*Young at Heart** (Arwin Production/
Warner Brothers Release, 1955).
Starred with Doris Day, Gig Young,
Ethel Barrymore & Dorothy Malone.
Not as a Stranger (Stanley Kramer
Production/United Artists Release,
1955). Starred with Olivia de
Havilland & Robert Mitchum.
*The Tender Trap** (MGM, 1955). Starred
with Debbie Reynolds, David Wayne &
Celeste Holm.
*Guys and Dolls** (Samuel Goldwyn
Production/MGM Release, 1955).
Starred with Marlon Brando, Jean
Simmons & Vivian Blaine.
The Man with the Golden Arm (Carlyle
Production/United Artists Release,
1955). Starred with Eleanor Parker &
Kim Novak.
Meet Me in Las Vegas (MGM, 1956). An
unbilled guest appearance.
Johnny Concho (Kent Production/
United Artists Release, 1956). Starred
with Keenan Wynn, William Conrad &
Phyllis Kirk. Also produced.
*High Society** (MGM, 1956). Starred
with Bing Crosby & Grace Kelly.
Around the World in 80 Days (Michael
Todd Production/United Artists
Release, 1956). Cameo as a piano
player in a Barbary Coast saloon.
The Pride and the Passion (Stanley
Kramer Production/Paramount
Release, 1957). Starred with Cary
Grant & Sophia Loren.
*The Joker Is Wild** (A.M.B.I.
Production/Paramount Release,
1957). Starred with Mitzi Gaynor,
Jeanne Crain & Eddie Albert.
*Pal Joey** (Essex-George Sidney
Production/Columbia Release, 1957).
Starred with Rita Hayworth & Kim
Novak.
Kings Go Forth (Frank Ross-Eton
Production/United Artists Release,
1958). Starred with Tony Curtis &
Natalie Wood.
Some Came Running (MGM, 1958).
Starred with Dean Martin, Shirley
MacLaine & Arthur Kennedy.
*A Hole in the Head** (Sincap Production/
United Artists Release, 1959). Starred
with Edward G. Robinson, Eleanor
Parker, Carolyn Jones & Keenan Wynn.
Never So Few (Canterbury Production/
MGM Release, 1959). Starred with
Gina Lollabrigida, Peter Lawford,
Steve McQueen, Richard Johnson,
Paul Henreid, Brian Donlevy & Dean
Jones.
*Can-Can** (Suffolk-Cummings
Production/Twentieth Century-Fox
Release, 1960). Starred with Shirley
MacLaine, Maurice Chevalier & Louis
Jourdan.
Ocean's Eleven (Dorchester Production/
Warner Brothers Release, 1960).
Starred with Dean Martin, Sammy

Davis Jr., Peter Lawford, Angie
Dickinson, Richard Conte, Cesar
Romero, Patrice Wymore, Joey
Bishop, Akim Tamiroff & Henry Silva.
Pepe (G.S. Posa Films International
Production/Columbia Release, 1960).
One of 27 personalities who appeared
as themselves.
The Devil at 4 O'Clock (Columbia, 1961).
Starred opposite Spencer Tracy.
Sergeants 3 (Essex-Claude Production/
United Artists Release, 1962). Starred
with Dean Martin, Sammy Davis Jr.,
Peter Lawford & Joey Bishop.
The Road to Hong Kong (Melnor Films
Production/United Artists Release,
1962). Appeared with Dean Martin as
guest artists.
The Manchurian Candidate (M.C.
Production/United Artists Release,
1963). Starred with Laurence Harvey,
Janet Leigh, Angela Lansbury, Henry
Silva, James Gregory & Leslie Parrish.
Come Blow Your Horn (Essex-Tandem
Production/Paramount Release,
1963). Starred with Lee J. Cobb,
Molly Picon, Barbara Rush, Jill St.
John & Tony Bill.
The List of Adrian Messenger (Joel
Production/Universal Release, 1963).
One of five stars who appeared in
disguise.
4 for Texas (Sam Company Production/
Warner Brothers Release, 1964).
Starred with Dean Martin, Anita
Ekberg, Ursula Andress, Charles
Bronson & Victor Buono.
*Robin and the Seven Hoods** (Warner,
1964). Musical gangster flick with
Bing Crosby, Dean Martin, Sammy
Davis Jr. & others.
The Oscar (Greene-Rouse Production/
Embassy Release, 1966). Appeared as
himself.
Assault on a Queen (Sinatra
Enterprises-Seven Arts Production/
Paramount Release, 1966). Starred
with Virna Lisi & Tony Franciosa.
The Naked Runner (Sinatra Enterprises
Production/Warner Brothers Release,
1967). Starring role.
Tony Rome (Arcola-Millfield Production/
Twentieth Century-Fox Release,
1967). Starring role.
The Detective (Arcola-Millfield
Production/Twentieth Century-Fox
Release, 1968). Starred with Lee
Remick.
Lady in Cement (Arcola-Millfield
Production/Twentieth Century-Fox
Release, 1968). Starring role.
Dirty Dingus Magee (MGM, 1970).
Starred with George Kennedy.
Contract on Cherry Street (Atlantis
Production/Columbia Release, 1977).
His first television movie (to be
shown abroad as a regular film).
Starred as a police inspector.
The First Deadly Sin (Atlantis-Cinema
VII Production/Filmways Release,
1980). Served as executive producer,
with Elliott Kastner. Starred opposite
Faye Dunaway.